The Rainmaker

The Rainmaker

Miracles and Healing Stories of
Om Swami

SADHVI VRINDA
SWAMI VEDANANDA & OTHERS

Published by
Rupa Publications India Pvt. Ltd 2021
161-B/4, Gulmohar House,
Yusuf Sarai Community Centre,
New Delhi 110049

Sales centres:
Bengaluru Chennai
Hyderabad Kolkata Mumbai

Copyright © Sadhvi Vrinda and Om Swami Vedananda 2021

All rights reserved.

The views and opinions expressed in this book are the authors' own and the facts are as reported by them which have been verified to the extent possible, and the publishers are not in any way liable for the same.

No part of this publication may be reproduced, transmitted, or stored in a retrieval system, in any form or by any means, electronic, mechanical, photocopying, recording or otherwise, without the prior permission of the publisher.

P-ISBN: 978-93-5520-140-9
E-ISBN: 978-93-5520-141-6

Ninth impression 2025

15 14 13 12 11 10 9

The moral right of the authors has been asserted.

Printed in India

This book is sold subject to the condition that it shall not, by way of trade or otherwise, be lent, resold, hired out, or otherwise circulated, without the publisher's prior consent, in any form of binding or cover other than that in which it is published.

The smile on your face
the shine in your eyes
as You stand amidst devotees
on the night of a full moon
bathed in fragrant unguents
oh water like pearls trickles
and drips
from your dark form
and like dirt to water
I run unto You
O Mother of three worlds
please take your child in
not battered as I once was
your grace has made me whole
On one hand, the joys of the world
on the other is You
serene
and safe...
just for a moment the world stops.
Let me in Mother
let me in on that tranquil state
of consciousness that flows
from your holy feet
to the bowed head of a devotee.
O Divine Mother
You are so beautiful
it breaks my heart
it aches
to be a part of You...

*Dedicated to the Divine Mother
with the deepest adoration*

Sudha-sindhor madhye sura-vitapi-vati parivrte
Mani-dweepe nipo'pavana-vathi chintamani-grhe;
Shivaakare manche Parama-Shiva-paryanka-nilayam
Bhajanti tvam dhanyah katichana chid-ananda-laharim.

In the middle of the sea of nectar
In the isle of precious gems
surrounded by the wish-giving Kalpaga trees
In the garden of Kadamba
In the house of the gem of thought
On the all-holy seat
the lap of the great Lord Shiva
She sits who is like a tide
in the sea of happiness of ultimate truth
And is worshipped by a few select holy ones.
(Verse 8, *Saundaraya Lahiri* by Adi Shankaracharya)

Contents

Mother Goddess	1
The Great Crumbling	7
Sickly Sweet	12
Mahayogi	22
Lifeline	55
The Blessing	91
Samadhi	103
Healing	118
At the Crown	139
My Master	144
The Mysterious Ways of the Universe	180
The End of a Sceptic	192
The Last Word–Sadhana	200
An Exclusive with Om Swami	207
Conversation with Om Swami	208

There is a deep realization that arises at some juncture in our lives that we don't really matter. I wish I could elaborate more on it but I doubt if there is much more to say. It's an unfamiliar feeling that I am a stranger to myself. In this endless sea of people, just another body gasping for air. Until, one day, when it all changes.

Mother Goddess

Have you seen how a puppy is hesitant and doubting of its new owner? As it settles in a bit, it starts to adore its mistress, jumping about, trailing after her wherever she goes. Sleeping on her shoes (shredding them to pieces when no one is looking), snuggling up to her at every opportunity, till they are inseparable. The puppy's adoration for its new-found mother is unmistakable. This is how I discovered the Goddess. The perfect Mother—gentle and giving.

The question then arises, is She real? One seldom questions the existence of the Creatress. We've grown up believing that She is real. But where is She? Is She in the Himalayas or far above the sky in an enchanted realm beyond our reach? In the ancient Vedic scriptures, famous texts are teeming with stories of the powerful Goddess who bestows great powers and is a constant companion to Her devout worshipper. Great Yogis, sages and poets have eulogized Her for eons as Mother of the Universe. In our culture, the oldest temples, rituals and prayers are built around the feminine principle, the Devi. She is considered both gentle and fierce, protector of truth and destroyer of all evil.

But what is the proof of Her existence, if there is one?

The image we have of Her in our mind is derived from the beliefs that already exist in society, in our parents' heads and in their altars. Is it merely our conditioned upbringing that strengthens our faith in Her, for who has ever seen Her? Except for a handful of venerable saints in the last few hundred years, no one can make claims to have realized Her form. And yet, millions of people pray to Her idol, worshiping the Devi in Her many different forms from the North to the South and the East to the West. To her devotee, She is real without a doubt.

The grace of Devi on Her bhaktas is perennial. She watches out for them and is never too far to hear their cries. This faith is passed on generation after generation as Ma's grace is felt and revered. And what of the one who renounces all worldly pleasures, becomes a mendicant meditating on Her glorious form, desperate to be one with Her? How does the merciful Mother reward a yogi's penance, who desires nothing but a union with Her pristine self? How does She manifest in him? The scriptures say, 'She becomes him.'

There is an odd analogy that comes to my mind. I once saw a few glasses next to a water dispenser. After someone used a glass, it was crushed and dumped in a nearby bin. A person came in, drank some water, squashed the glass and aimed it at the bin. He was in too great a hurry and the poor glass landed on the ground like an outcast. It wasn't even entitled its final resting place. In my mind, I wasn't too different from that crushed glass that had been used and tossed about. From that outcast disposable glass that was a hazard to the environment and had no use left in it, to becoming a sannyasin, life couldn't get more beautiful or dramatic than this.

The grace of the Divine Mother led me to my guru's door, who straightened every mark, every crease on the glass and set me back on the shelf, all shiny and new, ready to be of use. We are all like those throwaway glasses that will one day end up in the death-bin, but until that happens, life must be lived fully. And no one is better equipped to guide us through this confusing maze called life than a self-realized guru.

If anyone told me a decade ago that one day, I would derive the greatest pleasure from praying to Divine Mother by serving the cause of my guru, I would have laughed my head off. The closest I knew of praying was to fold my hands in front of an idol. I don't remember bowing in front of any living entity. I had nothing against it; it's just that no one ever evoked such emotions in my heart.

But then again, my guru says, when truth knocks, it knocks down.

When Mother Divine filled the cup of my life, I realized why millions pray to Her and why some of the greatest sages of the past eulogized Her.

On this Earth, She walks and flows through the speech and conduct, blessings and grace of yogis, tapasvis and saints. He who has Her favour is venerated as Mother himself. Alistair Shearer in his book, *In the Light of the Self: Adi Shankara and the Yoga of Non-dualism,* narrates a beautiful tale from the extraordinary childhood of the holy sage Adi Guru Shankaracharya:[*]

As it happened, the place belonged to a couple that

---

[*]Alistair Shearer, *In the Light of the Self: Adi Shankara and the Yoga of Non-dualism*, White Crow Books, 2017.

everyone knew weren't worth a turmeric root. Their ungrateful children had left home long since and they were living out their declining years in poverty, alone and unaided.

Each year, almost as soon as their meagre crops began to sprout, a flock of screeching green parrots would descend to nip each bud in the field with their razor-sharp bills, or a band of chattering monkeys would swing down from the high branches of the great banyan to take the unripe fruit from their few spindly papaya trees.

Yet, despite their misfortunes, the couple were unfailingly pious and humble, and the villagers were dismayed that such good people should suffer this undeserved hardship. Once, after a rock fell inexplicably on their roof on the night of no moon, it was generally agreed that the old couple must be possessed by a *chatan*, a possessing spirit

Several of the wealthier members of the village got together and decided to hire the services of an *ashtavaidya* skilled in dealing with such spirits. He duly came all the way from Trichur, bringing with him a copper-bound clay pot containing ten-year-old *ghee* fortified by herbs and empowered by mantras to the Goddess and Ganesh.

He talked gently to the couple, recited sacred verses and tied the protective black thread round their wrists; he performed *puja* with special incense beneath the old *peepal* tree where the *chatan* was probably living. But it was all to no avail. Their crops continued to suffer and their fortunes to decline.

Knowing all this, the boy, Shankara's initial reaction

was to pass by the house and continue down to the next, but something drew him to the dilapidated door. The woman of the house answered his call and her face lit up to see the little *brahmachari* standing there, but her pleasure at being asked to donate to a bowl of such good repute turned rapidly to embarrassment. There was no food in the house. Explaining that her husband was at that moment foraging for some leaves in the forest, she went back inside to return a few minutes later with all that she had: a single shriveled *amalaka* fruit.

Lowering her eyes in shame, she placed the fruit in the bowl and putting her thin hands together in salutation, bowed down. The boy felt overwhelmed at such devotion.

He closed his eyes and a silent prayer to Lakshmi, the Goddess of Abundance, rose up from his heart:

> Oh Mother Lakshmi, energy of the Divine, may your compassionate gaze become the clouds and your grace become the wind, and let them together pour down rain to extinguish the flames of this poor woman's *karmas*. May your celestial rain shower riches over this sorrowful little bird of yours!
>
> (Verse 8 of the *Khanaka-dhara-stava*, the hymn to Lakshmi traditionally said to be Shankara's first composition.)

No one knows just what happened next, but it is said the woman remembered everything around her dissolving into a brilliant light and an overwhelming sense of softness and delicacy, the very essence of femininity, sweeping over her.

The light intensified, and then from the densest point at its centre appeared the form of the goddess Lakshmi. She was huge and radiant, with an expression of indescribable sweetness, and two of her hands held a lotus flower. From another of her hands a stream of gold came forth, bubbling and glittering. At this point the old woman lost consciousness. When she came to, both the Goddess and the boy had gone, but the ground around her was heaped with gold coins.

The proof of the Divine Mother's existence is as much in lore and fables, as in the unique grace that transforms the shabby, pitiful life of a devotee, a disciple, into a golden life of wisdom and meaning under the tutelage of the guru. It's the same light I've often found myself gaping at—the radiance of Devi and the brilliance of Shankara—in my guru. A multitude of prayers have passed from Swamiji's lips to the Mother Goddess, to elevate those who seek his refuge. It's hard to ignore, when the events are unfolding right in front of you.

In my master's occult powers—that he denies and hides—in his gentle demeanour and in the blessings that flow from him, Ma is ever-present. From Swamiji's graceful gait, his pink and fair colouring, to his kind speech, all-knowing eyes and wish-fulfilling ways, he is the Divine Mother to us.

This book is dedicated to my guru's divine constant companion, the Devi.

The Great Crumbling

It was the month of July in 2020, and the rains hadn't yet begun. It was my fortieth year, and I wondered what more this decade would bring. While we were safe in my master's divine shade, the world all around us was crumbling. Economies were toppling, international waters remained closed, borders were sealed, mankind and womankind were chained to iPad screens and kitchen sinks. A tiny virus had brought great and small nations to their knees. The full horror of COVID-19 would probably be realized once we truly had a chance to catch our breath.

At the ashram, however, not much had changed, from pizza to panini, long river walks to open skies, the cool shade of the trees and ringing laughter, our lives remained unaffected. Devotional singing, chanting, spiritual practices and the occasional skirmishes went on as before. Often, waking up to the white mist settled on mountain tops, my heart longed to run to the temple compound to watch the pink Sun cracking through the clouds, smell the flowers on the way and inhale the scent of the wet earth.

There was the occasional disruption when the power went out and some of us cribbed about the humidity in the air, negligence of the local electricity supply and our rickety transformer. A little too much chilli in the ashram dining hall was the next grave source of discomfort to some. Other than that, there was not even the tiniest sign of anything even remotely disturbing. That a virus was raging in the world outside and taking lives was inconceivable. We were not even required to wear masks. It was as if we were one giant family living in a different world. If I could paint for you, my dear reader, a picture of our little paradise, it would be something like this. Have you seen how a beach by the ocean is abuzz with bodies young and old? How tiny, opaque shells rest about as crabs scuttle out of the broken ones, and happy little creatures burrow their heads in the sand?

Then there were the fish in the sea, big and small, schools of them. The dolphins, sharks, whales, preying on the smaller fish. Clams and algae and millions of other life forms swimming in the sea, surviving, dying and being born again. The green-blue waters of the high seas mirrored our own chaotic world.

And yet, at the bottom of the sea, in the great depths of the ocean, all was silent. Still. Restful. Why wouldn't it be? It's the abode of the great Lord Narayana, as He reclines on His serpent bed, asleep yet awake. He who sustains the three worlds. It's His abode, Vaikuntha, a place without suffering that our master had carved for us in Sri Badrika ashram. Immune from real sorrow or loss, we lived in the ashram, safe from *the great crumbling*. Our petty grumbling was no match for what was out there enfeebling the world.

'I don't tell, I just do.'

These words resonated in my mind as I sat in the ashram library, facing the bright orange temple flag. The green lawn, lush with tiny blades of recently mowed grass, bore witness to the serene lap of Mother Nature I found myself in.

Swamiji had slipped away into his solitude for an unknown period. We were used to his frequent disappearances into silence. Just as there are different seasons in a year—Autumn, Spring, Summer, there's *Solitude*; it was just another season for us. This season of separation from our master had over time become a hallowed period where some of us took on vows of silence for a while to purify our minds and speech, while working on bettering ourselves. Just as the Sun slips behind the clouds and yet continues to brighten the sky, making it mysteriously breathtaking, the distance from our great master lit up our soul even more.

Many evenings, while walking in the temple garden, I'd see flocks of tiny birds, the size of my thumb, flapping their wings from one tall tree to another. The wind was not to be left behind and she would assume the form of a cloud-maiden who swooshes about juggling fallen leaves in the air. The skyline was marked by mountains greener than green. In the twilight of a purple and violet sky, it was a sight to behold. A sweet longing would rise in the heart to revere my master. And I'd request the wind and the birds to carry my message to him, knowing well that that they would. It's more poetic than shooting a practical email sometimes.

Once, we were having a residents' meeting. A few residents had some personal issues, and everyone was trying to tell Swamiji their version of what had conspired. He simply raised a gentle hand in the air and said in a serious tone, 'Please, there's no need to tell me what's happening in the ashram, either by addressing emails to me or by sending handwritten notes. All that I need to know, I know. The birds tell me everything I need to know.'

Sitting in the first row, my ears piqued like a dog's, for I had heard of this for the very first time. Everyone around sat quietly, taking in the impact of what our guru had just said. We all knew that Swamiji only spoke the truth, and if he said the birds told him everything, then it had to be true. The next day, I couldn't resist asking him about it. I prided myself in knowing much about his mystical side and was quite intrigued that something so important had remained hidden in plain sight from me.

'Swamiji, yesterday, you said the birds tell you everything. In all these years, you've never once mentioned about the birds,' I persisted, 'Why did you never tell me?'

'I couldn't,' he said grinning at Swami Vidyananda (Vidya Swami), almost winking, 'I knew you'd slip it in your book.'

And that has always been a joke amongst the three of us. Swamiji would always caution Swami Vidyananda to be careful about what they spoke around me, for before they knew it, I'd make a mental note to add it to a book. On a serious note, it has always been his endeavour to equip people to lead their lives practically, through hard work and resilience. Mysticism is something he has neither promoted nor preached. And yet, as his disciples, we know, having borne witness to miracles on innumerable occasions, that there is no end to what he can do, should he choose to.

You just have to spend a few days in the ashram to know what I mean. Among other things, here is a place that has all the opulence and amenities, built as if magically. Except for a small fundraising campaign of a few lakh rupees to build a place for Sri Hari, he has never appealed for funds or given any VIPs any special treatments and yet, everything is available here. In fact, we have more comforts here than in our homes. When 10 years ago, Swamiji came and sat down in a tiny mud hut, devotees tell me that he had said, 'You can't even imagine what this place is going to be in just a few years from now. Mother Goddess walks here.'

Sickly Sweet

It's a kind of a rule of writing that the written word be given a title. An article must have a header and a name. You can do away with chapter titles if you like, but the goddamn book needs to have a titillating name. What about feelings, do they have headings? Need they be categorized? Sure, if you are in therapy.

So, I asked myself this, must I give an absolute name to my deep awe and reverence for my master's wisdom and power? Can the divine dance of his grace not be sung in undertones? It's possible, perhaps, but not many know what I know. A few years ago, I came across this Amazon review of my first book on Swamiji, *Om Swami: As We Know Him*.

> This book comes across as a sincere attempt by Om Swami's disciples to express their guru bhakti. This is no fault of the authors (because each of us has our own style of expression) but the book is very heavy with metaphors and similes that often distract one from the message they appear to be trying to get across i.e. that their guru is God manifest (which of course is the case with all true Gurus in the world).

The style of writing is sincere but very **sickly sweet** most of the time (almost nauseating at times). I read this book right after the book *Radha: Diary of a Woman's Search* by a disciple of Swami Sivananda (of Divine Life Society, Rishikesh).

The contrast in the writing could not be greater— Radha writes in a down-to-earth way with no embellishments, yet her devotion to her guru and his greatness is absolutely clear. Each to their own, I guess. May God bless the authors and us all.

When I first read this review, I couldn't help but smile. 'Sickly sweet'—I knew what the reviewer meant. I understood her cynicism. For I too, was an infiltrator once and had lived across the border. The border of scepticism. In my shabby little hut of ignorance, I had perceived spirituality to be confined to self-help books and writings of or on long-dead realized saints.

Truth is, most of us have never experienced the heart-melting kindness and peace one experiences bowing at the holy feet of a saint. Nothing written in a book, no matter how beautiful or lyrical, can prepare us for the cooling effect of their divine presence. It's as if for a moment your life stands still. You are hopeful like a child as to what great things might tumble out of the enlightened being in front of you, changing your life forever. It's what happened to me and not a day goes by when I don't thank Bhagwan for the sublime advent of my guru in my life.

In the early days, I wondered, how could anyone be so kind or speak so gently all the time? Didn't he ever get tired of being nice to *everyone*? He'll surely crack one day, be unkind to me or the hordes of people who throng to him. There must be a flaw, a display of selfishness that'll give him away. It came naturally to me to doubt anyone who possessed virtues of kindness and empathy, for, in our world, they usually amount to play pretend. It felt unreal to see someone so noble and, at the time, it even made me angry.

But just as time reveals the nature of all things, my awe increased multifold. Eight dreamlike years later, his many powers continue to bewilder and baffle me. What do you do when your master not only has the power to know your mind effortlessly but to see and hear you, wherever you are? No doors, walls, distances between countries and continents can stop him from knowing about the well-being of those who depended on him. I don't think they have made the kind of telescopes or microscopes that can allow a person to look into someone's core and see their life's journey in less than the time it takes to join one's hands. I had long ago concluded that there was no hiding from him. I know I make it sound like I'm a rat caught in a lab experiment, but remember, my writing style is 'heavy with metaphors and similes.'

And if all this is still not enough to overwhelm you, your guru heals your loved one from a strange brain fever. A strange case, where even the best doctors in Europe can't figure out the cause, despite four lumbar punctures (and eight weeks in the hospital). Then there is his name, which by simply uttering it over a glass of plain water and giving it to your blind, dying dog, not only restores her vision but keeps her alive for over a year, until you are ready to bear her passing. Who today in this world can claim to do all this? So please don't mind me if I can't keep my zeal from spilling onto these pages.

My devotion isn't devotion at all, it's pure awe, raw astonishment and wonder at how my master does what he does.

Sickly sweet, it might get for some of you, but it doesn't change the truth. You always have the option to dismiss it as a story, but imagine what you'd lose out on the path of spirituality if you discover that he actually turns out to be who I say he is. Penning down this line really made me laugh; I hope you see the humour in it too.

A day before Swamiji's journey into solitude, Swami Vidyananda and I sat by his feet, trying to hold on to the last few hours. I felt voiceless inside. A strange fear gripped my heart. Sensing my unquiet spirit, he placed his hand gently on my head. I closed my eyes. A beautiful energy flowed from his palm to my head, lifting my consciousness instantly. It was no different from flicking on a light switch. While his hand was on my head, I sneaked a look at Swamiji's face and found him murmuring a chant. Opening his gentle eyes, he stilled my shifty movements with a glance and closed his eyes again.

His lips were still moving, and I thought to myself, *'It's quite a long blessing.'*

When he finished a few seconds later, I asked him, 'What blessing did you give me, Swamiji?'

'Always asking Bauji (father) questions,' retorted Swami Vidyananda.

Shushing him with a look, I asked him, 'Please tell us. You never tell us anything.'

Laughing, Swamiji leaned back in the soft grey recliner.

'I don't tell, I just do.'

Smiling, I put my hands up in surrender. '*Yes*,' I thought to myself, '*he just does.*' To give you context, a long-time ardent devotee was diagnosed with cancer. He met Swamiji on a sacred Hindu festival and told him that he wasn't sure if he was going to live to see the next year's festival. The cancer was at an advanced stage. Swamiji asked him to continue to explore alternate treatments and said that he was there with him. Swamiji opened the door to go out, as Swami Vidyananda stood waiting outside. But then he closed the door a bit, turned around, and gave the man a hug. 'Not so soon, not yet. I'll protect you,' Vidya Swami heard Swamiji saying these words to the man.

Rather than walk out of the meeting room, Swamiji sent the man away and waved at Vidya Swami.

'Bauji,' Vidya Swami said, 'this must be a very special case for the man to receive a hug from you.'

'I need to save him at this time,' was all Swamiji said.

Suddenly, Vidya Swami realized that Swamiji was shivering. These were winter months; the heater was on, and yet, it was unusual for Swamiji to feel cold, let alone shiver with cold. In the last seven years, it was the first time he had seen the master shiver.

Vidya Swami always tells us that Swamiji's body has too much heat due to samadhi (meditation) and other yogic practices—whether hot or cold, hail or snow, cotton robes are all he wears round the year. He was immediately concerned at finding his master freezing. His health continued to slide over the next few weeks. Since we have always seen Swamiji unwell, with one thing or the other, this was just another incident in a long list of incidents that faded away with time. I'd liken it to having a sick child at home. There's relief from one ailment and then something else comes up, as there's always someone in queue, waiting to be healed. It's how I've always seen my master, his health tender and delicate. Three years later, the said devotee whom Swamiji had blessed continues to enjoy good health.

While writing this book with Swami Vidyananda, he reminded me of this incident and how these repeated interferences in nature's cycle has weakened Bauji's immunity. Everything comes at a price. It's also true that if people have returned from the verge of death, there are those who haven't. In a detached but loving manner, Swamiji always reminds us that not all can be saved. *The laws of karma can be bent, they can't be broken.*

'We must leave the outcome to the Divine Mother. She balances the karmic cycle and it's Her will alone that prevails,' he often tells us.

'But how long will you continue to pay the price of others' karma?'

'I have to do what I can for them...they have invested their faith in me.' Before I can open my mouth to protest, he is already humming a bhajan, increasing the tempo as he sings. It's how Swamiji shuts me up most of the times, especially when he doesn't wish to address my questions. It's endearing to see him dodge my queries with a devotional tune or a spur-of-the-moment song to make us laugh. Sometimes, out of the blue, he even surprises us with an old movie number. And so, what begins as a serious discussion on my part, ends up being funny. I think, if Swamiji wasn't a saint, he would have made a great comedian too.

As I mull over how to best introduce that hidden side of my guru that cures and heals, these words continue to reverberate in my head,

'I don't tell, I just do.'

~

In the winter of 2018, a man from a small town came to visit Swamiji. He spoke in a dialect native to Uttarakhand and was in his mid-30s. His name was Babloo. I heard from Swami Vedananda (not to be confused with Swami Vidyananda), Swamiji's very efficient personal assistant (PA), that the new guest needed to be looked after well. The best river-facing room was given to Babloo and his companion. Swamiji was quite pleased to have him in the ashram. There was a constant smile on his face when he spoke of the time spent with Babloo in the Himalayas.

Since I'm always keen on meeting people who knew my guru from the time he spent in intense penance in the Himalayas, I requested Swami Vedananda to arrange a meeting with our special guest. He was polite and well-dressed, yet he had that rustic look that comes from growing up in a small town. Babloo bore a striking resemblance to the popular Sufi singer, Kailash Kher. He even spoke like him, in that beautiful nasal voice. It tickled my funny bone. I asked Babloo why it had taken him so long to come and see Swamiji in the ashram.

Pointing to his friend, who sat snuggled in a white quilt, he said, 'My friend Bhim Singh gave me Swamiji's memoir, *Satya Kahoon Toh* (the Hindi edition of *If Truth Be Told*) last month and I was shocked.'

'Shocked?' I said. 'Why?'

'Why hasn't Maharaj-ji written anything about himself in the book?'

'What do you mean?' I said, quite perplexed. 'The whole memoir is about him.'

'No, it isn't. Maharaj-ji hasn't mentioned any of the miracles he regularly performed when he was with us, Sadhviji. There's so much more to him than just what is in the book.'

I was a bit taken aback, as here I was, Swamiji's personal editor and disciple, and this simple, unassuming man claimed to know more than all of us put together.

'I'll write a book on Maharaj-ji, a tell-all—the memoir barely scratches the surface of his intense yogic powers.'

I could barely contain my excitement and curiosity and immediately asked Babloo to tell me more, as we shared the same passion—to sing our guru's glories.

'I recently compiled the Book of Faith exactly for the same reason. Our guru is so much more...'

Babloo was happy to hear about the new book but sad because it was in English and there was no Hindi translation yet. I urged him to tell me his story and that I'd be happy to pen it down for him.

Swami Vedananda and I sat in rapt attention for the next hour as Babloo told us one hair-raising story after another. It was like hearing about a different person altogether. Swamiji had from time to time blessed me with many glimpses of his divine and mystical side but listening to these stories, I could only think, 'How well do I really know my master?'

I recorded them all and made backups as I didn't want to lose my new-found treasure to a technical glitch. I've shared some of the stories in this book, the rest are for another time, another book. There's only so much of a dose of divinity our mortal, questioning minds can take, right?

The next morning, filled with even more awe than before, I bowed to my guru, who sat enjoying the peaceful post-breakfast silence. I, on the other hand, was burning with curiosity.

'Oh Swamiji, I met Babloo last night. He told us so many stories from your time at Anasuya temple, Rudranath and the woods...why did you help him so much?'

'He had no agenda of his own when he made arrangements for my sadhana (spiritual practice). He did it selflessly,' Swamiji smiled, quite certain that my questions had only just begun. The light ochre of the robe matched his perfectly clear and radiant face. His sharp nose reminded me of a red-beaked parrot perched on a ripened mango tree. For a moment, I forgot all about my carefully prepared questions and just basked in his tender, mischievous smile.

As I sat there speechless, he shook his head to the side indicating that I better be on my way, as he had work to do. I quickly straightened myself and said, 'Just one thing, Swamiji. Why do you help people that no one knows? If you helped rich and famous people, at least then they would go and tell other people who you are, and we wouldn't have to worry about ashram upkeeps and finances.'

Swamiji started laughing at my silliness and said, 'Look around you, do you think we lack anything? Mother Divine herself is seated in our sanctum sanctorum. She blesses us with everything we could possibly need.' It's true, we, the disciples lack nothing. We own the best of gadgets, comforts and luxuries, thanks to our guru's ever-flowing generosity.

'But why don't you help rich people?' I persisted.

'We do help them, but the rich forget. When they are in trouble—financial, professional, health or in any other crisis, they knock on our door. After their work is done with divine intervention, they attribute it to other factors. Not all of course, but most do it.' He paused for a moment to run a hand on his round head and said, 'They seldom feel comfortable sharing with other educated minds how dharma saved their business, cured an illness, saved their marriage or child, and so on.'

'So, why do we help them?'

He chuckled. 'Samoaham sarva-bhuteshu na me dveshyoasti na priayah...all are equal for me. I've no personal favourites nor do I despise anyone. And remember, Sadhviji, as saints, we at all times have to do our dharma. That's all that matters.'

And so, as a disciple, it's not only my dharma to sing my Guru's praise, it's all that I know. His miracles are many. Dare I capture them in words?

Sometimes, I ask myself, if it's merely the devotion of a disciple, the blind faith of a devotee or the fascination of love, it'll surely ebb and flow. It doesn't. It's a song that plays over and over in the hidden cove of my soul. It lingers. It replays. It murmurs. Steady like a rock, it never wavers; earthquakes of emotions play hide-and-seek, and yet devotion stays put.

All the worldly relationships I've known are long lost and forgotten. Only the loving face of my master and the Divine Mother are etched in the deep furrows of my mind. In this small and inglorious life of mine, my guru, with his kindness and laughter, has saved me repeatedly.

This mouth never tires of singing his glories. Just as Babloo could only stare in disbelief on reading the memoir, I too am in perpetual awe of my modest master. These words continue to ring in my ears, 'I don't tell, I just do'.

Mahayogi

Babloo

There is not much to say about me. I'm in the construction business and my parents have a humble residence in the temple premises of the revered Anasuya Mata shrine in a village called Mandal in Uttarakhand. For many generations, our family has been the custodian of the sanctum shrine and in our joint family, the men take turns to be the pujaris (priests)—one year, it would be my father's turn, and in the next, my uncle's. Even though I was brought up in a deeply religious environment, the job of a temple priest did not appeal to me much. I did not feel I was qualified enough to take on that responsibility.

Mandal falls under the Chamoli district. The nearest town is Gopeshwar, which is some 15 kilometres away, and there are a couple of buses that run from there to our village. Most people, however, take shared taxis, usually Boleros or Tata Sumos, as they tend to be cheaper and faster. Every year, tens of thousands of devotees flock to the Anasuya temple, which is famous for granting the boon of a child to childless couples. In fact, we have a wildly popular annual two-day fair inaugurated by a state minister, sometimes the chief minister himself, and is attended by a few thousand devotees who visit us from all parts of the country. The couples who get blessed with a child after visiting the temple, particularly make it a point to come back with their families to pay homage to the Goddess. Being the temple priest of such an ancient temple is an honour anyone in my village would die for. But I was 24 years old at the time, and had great ambition. So I convinced my father to bid for a government tender involving the renovation of the temple. It was a big project. We had some experience in the construction business, but not a great deal of it.

However, in 2010, the project had been delayed due to completely unforeseen issues and God had brought me to my knees. I felt terrible all the time for having pushed my family into financial ruin. Not only would we gain nothing from the project, we would actually lose, because in my zest we had severely underestimated the costs. I had become the laughing stock of the village, the black sheep of the family. I was told by the department that if the project wasn't completed on time, my father and I would be blacklisted from bidding on any future projects, forever. The situation became so terrible that for four months we bought groceries on credit. We didn't need much, just rice and lentils, but we didn't have the money. It was my father's turn to be the priest that year so there was some income from the temple, but all of it was going in the temple extension and renovation project. The department withheld our payments and told us our dues would only be released if we successfully finished the project.

We had never been so stressed. I was completely lost in the maze of simply making ends meet, redeeming my dignity and self-esteem, looking after our cattle, sourcing labour and materials and getting the construction done. I was so dejected that, at times, I thought of jumping from one of the cliffs I passed by on a daily basis on my temple-village trek. There is no motorable road to our home or the temple. When you get down at Mandal, you have to undertake a five-kilometre trek to reach the temple. I often marvel at the tourists and travellers who come to Uttarakhand for trekking. Why on earth would they roam up and down the mountains if they aren't doing it for themselves or their cattle? How lucky were these people? They didn't have to spend three hours on an arduous terrain just to buy a bottle of kerosene oil.

So in 2010, I saw no light at the end of the tunnel and stood to suffer from much more than financial ruin. Public humiliation awaited us. Less than four months away was the big day of the fair and the temple renovation was not even 40 per cent done. Other than the entire flooring and walls, two giant roofs had to be put in place. Forget pouring and drying the concrete, even the iron mesh wasn't in place. One could only bring so much material to the construction site on ponies. The workers were giving us a really hard time. Some of them had now set conditions—they would only work if we provided meals as well. We didn't even have money to feed ourselves.

Every day I prayed to Mata Anasuya, our Kula Devi, to help me get through this. I did not want to bring more disrepute to my family. I rued the day I thought of taking on this project. And then, one fine day, completely unexpectedly,

I met Maharaj-ji, or as everyone called him, Swamiji. (In Uttarakhand, we address all venerable saints as Maharaj-ji.)

My first meeting with him, I'm ashamed to confess, began on the wrong foot. Every day, tens of sadhus and sannyasis visit our temple, and most of them are only there to get a free night's stay, a meal or something like that. I hope you won't judge me for saying this, but the more sadhus I met, the less I liked my religion. Most of the sadhus who trekked and travelled engaged in more ignoble acts than any other group of devotees. So when I saw this sadhu walk towards the temple (and I could only see his back), I thought here was one more sadhu who would now stop and engage in petty talk and waste my time. I saw that he stood near the temple. Due to the construction work, it looked like a war zone. Giant rocks, concrete, cement, sand, gravel, iron, nails and a lot of dust, everything just lay there.

I was angry anyway and, furthermore, I noticed that this sadhu was standing on the construction site with his shoes on. Though they were only made of cloth, and we all wore shoes too, somehow I thought this was a haughty person who did not respect the sanctity of the place.

Besides, my cousin had whispered in my ear, 'This guy is probably a phau-reigner (foreigner),' since he had caught a glimpse of him from a distance earlier. So, at the time, my judgement was rather clouded.

I shouted from behind, 'O Maharaj, can't you see where you are standing?'

I wasn't going to call anyone Maharaj-ji just because he wore saffron clothes.

He turned slowly, and the moment my gaze fell on his

face, my hands went up in the air. I can't explain that feeling, but I never expected to see such radiance on any human being's face. As far back as I could remember, having seen thousands of saints visit our temple, I never saw anyone with such extraordinary charisma and tej (radiance). I felt a little intimidated. But I wasn't giving up so fast. If you are a temple priest, you see all kinds of people all day. So my initial reaction was quickly clouded by doubt and disbelief.

'Arey, he looks like a real saint,' my cousin whispered in my ear. I just nodded, but a tinge of confusion still lingered in my head—was this particular 'Maharaj' from India and did he speak Hindi?

As he walked towards us, I said, 'Maharaj, where are you from? Tell us a bit about yourself.'

'Instead, why don't I tell you about you?' he countered.

Like a majestic king, he walked most gracefully and sat on one of the walls that had been half demolished. We just followed him like sheep and sat around the place.

'Ah, I see,' he said smiling. 'You are angry. Very angry. Your construction project is falling apart, you are losing money and, what's more, you are in pain. You can't sit.'

'What do you mean?' I asked.

'You know what I mean,' he said. 'You have a boil on your back and you can't sit.'

'Maharaj-ji. You are right.'

'You guys have promoted me very quickly,' he said.

We looked at him, utterly perplexed.

'I mean,' he continued, 'from "that guy", "Maharaj", to "Maharaj-ji"! All in a matter of a few minutes!'

'I'm in a lot of trouble, Maharaj-ji.'

'I told you that's because you can't sit. You took on this monster project, but you know you can't finish it. This is not just an albatross around your neck, it's a noose.'

He sat there and gave a detailed account of our past like he was reading from some book. We weren't just blown away, we were torn apart.

'Sorry, Maharaj-ji,' we both said. 'It's just that every day, sadhus and devotees visit us. We thought you were just like any other sadhu.'

He just smiled.

'Babloo,' My mother called out to me. 'Eat your lunch. It's getting cold.'

'Maharaj-ji,' I said, 'please have prasadam (sanctified food, later offered to devotees) at our place.'

'Only if you let me pay.'

I folded my hands and pleaded with him to accept my humble offering of a meal and not talk about paying.

'It's hard for me to make anyone understand this, Babloo,' he said, 'but I almost never accept offerings of any material nature. Because if I do, I'm obligated by nature to return the favour manifold in my own time, at my own pace.'

'That's all the more reason, Maharaj-ji,' I said. 'From your plumbless ocean, a few drops will wash away all my troubles. Even if not as a devotee, as a temple priest, let me host you. A Brahmin is requesting you.'

He smiled and looked up at the sky, his beautiful eyebrows arched, his radiant eyes exposed, and said, 'Okay.'

I took him to our modest dwelling, just a few steps away from the temple. When I say modest, I'm not trying to sound modest—it is actually a humble residence. Two tiny rooms and one small kitchen. Walls of mud painted with a mixture of cow dung and clay. My mother cooked on a wooden stove, and we would sit down on a wooden board to eat. At night, we would take out a thin mattress and make that our bed.

Maharaj-ji sat on the wooden board and I could not muster the courage to sit at the same level as him. I sat on the floor. My mother was sitting next to me, making hot chapatis. Maharaj-ji motioned me to come and sit on the board next to him. I couldn't do it. I folded my hands.

'This Maharaj-ji looks like a real tapasvi (ascetic),' my mother mumbled to me. I gave her a look, gesturing at her to not speak like that since he was sitting right there.

'Maharaj-ji,' my mother said, 'Babloo is 24 years old but it is the first time he has ever brought a sadhu home for a meal.'

'Thank you for feeding me, Ma,' Maharaj-ji said, 'I owe you and I'll make good of this debt.'

My mother said it was her honour but what struck me was how lovingly Maharaj-ji spoke. I don't remember anyone ever speaking to my mother so courteously. Not me, my siblings, father, cousins, visitors, other saints, no one. Not even one person. To be honest with you, it had never occurred to me that it was possible to speak to someone with such grace and humility.

My phone rang and I stepped out. I told Maharaj-ji to continue with his meal and that I would be back in a few minutes. My few minutes changed to some 20-odd ones. When I went back, he had finished his meal and was waiting for me to finish mine. I was quite distressed, though, and could not eat.

Three people from the government had dropped by and, in the harshest language, scolded me for not finishing the construction project on time. I was humiliated in front of my cousins, extended family, contractors and my deity. They threatened to get an advertisement out in the next day's paper stating that my company was blacklisted from undertaking any further projects in the area. Ultimately, this also meant that the entire business would then go to my competitor. I was a simple thekedaar, a contractor—no business meant no work and no livelihood.

The chief minister's PA had called the district magistrate confirming his attendance for this year's fair. Everyone was under a lot of pressure. People were worried that they would perhaps lose their jobs if the temple wasn't completely ready on time. There were others, jealous people, who were waiting for me to fail, anyway. Many of my well-wishers who had advised me against taking on this project, would routinely call my father to rub it in.

I had tried to take the government officials away from the scene, but they kept on humiliating me with a steady stream of expletives. I am sure Maharaj-ji and everyone around us had heard them loud and clear. Thankfully, my father was not home at the time as he had gone to Gopeshwar to convince some labourers to work on our project.

They turned down all my entreaties, vented to their heart's content, took out all their frustration on me and went away. I quickly came back to the room as standing among all those people was unbearable. I told my mother that I didn't want to finish the rest of the meal. A tear escaped my eye.

'Babloo,' Maharaj-ji said as I stared at the ground. 'Look at me.'

I raised my head a little.

'The very people who have insulted you, will call you tonight. First, they'll apologize for their behaviour, and second, within two days, they'll bring their own labour and lay the foundation of the roof.'

I was surprised to hear what he was saying and was unsure how to react. I was extremely disturbed, and found myself clinging to Maharaj-ji because there was a strange solace in his company. I just wanted to be around him and hear his voice. Soon after lunch, my cousin Vinod and I asked a question we should have asked two hours ago.

'What brings you to Anasuya temple, Maharaj-ji?'

He shared that he had been meditating in a cave in Badrinath but that people had found out about that cave. As a result, every other day, someone or the other would knock on his cave's door. So he was looking for a really secluded spot that was hard to reach, somewhere he could meditate in peace. He mentioned that he had heard about Atri Muni's cave and that he was keen to see it.

We told him that the Atri Muni cave was one of the most sacred and secluded places around here and that we had never let any sadhu stay there overnight. However, we would not only make an exception for him but turn the heavens upside down to try our best to provide for him, no matter what he needed. Immediately, we made our way to the cave. It was a 30-minute trek from our temple, and you had to practically lie flat and slide through a thin crevice to enter the place. Once near the cave, there was ample space for one person, with a giant waterfall nearby.

'How will we get any supplies through that crevice?' he asked.

We showed him a roundabout way to approach the cave. According to our religious beliefs, one could enter from only one particular side of the crevice, but supplies could actually be delivered from the other side.

Maharaj-ji told us that he would need to meditate there for an indefinite period of time and that once a month, or even once every three months, we could just ensure that rice and lentils reached him. A gas cylinder would easily last three months.

'I will only eat once a day. A handful of rice,' he said. 'So provisions will last me a long time.'

The only issue was that once every year, for two days, thousands of people came for a pilgrimage, and so he would be disturbed for those two days. The rest of the year, we would ensure that no one else visited the cave. Maharaj-ji told us that his sadhana would be well under way at that time and he wouldn't want a break, but since there was no other option, he would accept this condition. He said he would structure his sadhana so that his main meditation would only start after the fair ended. I didn't understand what he meant, but all I knew was that this location could work for him. And I, on my part, wanted to do whatever I could to ensure that Maharaj-ji could stay there.

He asked us about the rent and we told him that there was no need for any, just his blessings were enough. He said he would need a wooden board to sleep on, a small gas stove and at least a makeshift door on the cave, so that he could meditate in peace. And, of course, two blankets—one to spread on the wooden board and the other to cover his body. We told him that he would need more than two blankets because there was no provision of firewood there and that snowfall was not uncommon in that area. He seemed to be okay with anything, really. We estimated that the cost for doing all that would be around ₹8,000. He handed us ₹15,000 and said that he would go back to Rishikesh the next day, where his luggage was, and would return within five days. We promised we would get everything done in a week so that when he returned, he could start with his sadhana.

I did not want to take any money from him, but I was struggling financially and I couldn't even provide the most basic amenities. We did offer him a room at the temple compound, but he said he needed complete seclusion.

When we got back to the temple, Maharaj-ji once again pointed at a distant mountain. He had done that just before we left for the cave, too. This was a place called Doghra. It was deep in the woods and was six kilometres away from our temple. There was no set trek. Only a local could get you through the dense forest infested with bears, boars and other wild animals. Leopards and tigers were a routine sighting in that region. Even though I was born and brought up in the same region, I had not been to Doghra more than a couple of times.

'That place is calling me, Babloo,' he said. 'That's where I need to be for my sadhana.'

We dissuaded him from going there and told him that the cave was his best option because, every now and then, we could go and check up on him and provide necessities. He agreed, even if he didn't seem convinced.

We allotted a room to Maharaj-ji in the temple dharamshala, and in the evening, I invited him back to my home for supper.

I had hardly eaten a handful of rice when my phone rang. It was from a government official. Once again, I stepped out. I knew what humiliation awaited me. The executive engineer was on the line, the same person who had verbally abused me in the afternoon.

'Samvaalji,' he said to me, 'we are sorry for using such harsh words with you at the temple compound. Please forgive our mistake. We are under a lot of pressure because CM sahib will be inaugurating the fair this year, and everything has to be made ready. It's been decided that we'll bring in some outside labour, and you bring in your men. We'll start laying the foundation of the roof of that section of the temple in the next couple of days.'

I could hardly contain my joy as I ran to Maharaj-ji's side to tell him what had just happened. He smiled sweetly and said, 'The people who walked up five kilometres to curse you today, will be walking five kilometres up again tomorrow to get your work going. They were here for 15 minutes. Let them now spend 150 hours going up and down.'

The next day, Maharaj-ji left for Rishikesh to get his bag and we were entrusted with the task of getting his cave ready. I am not sure how to tell you this, but I couldn't do anything at all in the next seven days. The people from the department came, and our entire focus was to just somehow get the work started. But it rained every single day. Our work could not commence and I couldn't do anything about the cave. Seven days later, Maharaj-ji returned and I was ashamed to even face him.

Vinod and I apprised him of the situation—absolutely nothing was ready. He chuckled, saying it was divine will and asked us to take him to the other location in the woods, the one he had been referring to from day one. I excused myself because I had to go and source material for our construction project the next day. Vinod agreed to take Maharaj-ji to show the location. Although we knew that there was no way he could stay in that wilderness, with absolutely no human contact, we agreed to do as he asked because he was so insistent.

The next day when I met Vinod and Maharaj-ji, he told us that it had been love at first sight and that he was certain he wanted to do his sadhana in the woods. The primary issue was that there was no water near that location. He asked me to contact someone who would pass on the message to a Pradeep Brahmachari. It was time for Brahmachari to be at his service, Maharaj-ji said. I called the number, and they said that Pradeep had already boarded his train from Brahmapur, Odisha, and was on his way to Uttarakhand.

'What is this magic, Maharaj-ji?' I asked as I came back in the room and told him the whole story. 'Does he know where you are?'

'I haven't spoken to him after I left Jagannath Puri, which was at least 10 days ago, but that doesn't mean Mother Divine can't arrange for him to be here when he's needed.'

We had a hearty meal at my home. Some devotees and my cousin and I sat in Maharaj-ji's room as he launched into a riveting discourse. To attend a live sermon by him, I say it without the slightest exaggeration, was one of the most memorable experiences of my life.

The next day, at lunch, Maharaj-ji was sitting in my home when three ladies arrived at our doorstep. My mother wanted them to seek his blessings. Divorce was imminent, he said to one of them. He blessed a fruit and gave it to the second one, for she had been unable to conceive for years, despite faithfully visiting the temple twice a year. Next year, she would not visit the temple empty-handed, he said to her. Maharaj-ji gently chided the third one and told her to not be so jealous and think ill of her in-laws all the time. He couldn't help her, he said.

Let me mention here, that one year later, when the second lady came back, she had a beautiful, plump baby in her arms. The first lady was divorced and had come looking for Maharaj-ji, and I don't know what became of the third one.

Presently, I went to his room and said, 'Maharaj-ji, the owners of those huts are not willing to come or talk. They don't want to rent out their huts to anyone.'

'Why? Is anyone staying there?'

'No one stays there in the winters. It snows there and the temperature becomes sub-zero.'

'So what's the problem?'

'Everything is a problem for them. It's better if you take up the cave because we can manage everything there.'

'Babloo,' he said softly, 'once I've decided something, nothing and no one stands between me and my goals. They will not only agree to come here and talk but they will also rent out their place. Call them again, and tell them that I have said so.'

I went out and called them to convey the message.

'What is the need, Maharaj-ji?'

'Need for what?'

'For you to do any sadhana? You already have so much

power. More power than anyone else I have ever seen. Why don't you live comfortably?'

He had a hearty laugh before he said, 'I'm not doing it for any power or siddhi, Babloo. I'm doing it to merge with God, to test the limits of my body and consciousness, to purify myself beyond what is humanly possible.'

He said some other things that I don't remember, but what I do recall is that I couldn't help but bow down and seek blessings of this being in front of me. I wish everyone has the good fortune of experiencing Maharaj-ji from such close quarters. I can't predict what you would feel, but I can tell you that it would be unlike any other experience you might have ever had.

While I was in Maharaj-ji's company, my phone rang again and I excused myself to take the call. After I returned, he said to me, 'The girl you were speaking to over the phone, she's the one you'll get married to.'

'Maharaj-ji, you are not messing with me, are you?' I was still wondering how he even knew I was speaking to a girl, when he said, 'You can have it in writing if you like, Babloo. She's going to be your wife. And she's a good person.'

In the evening, the owners of the Doghra huts came and not only did they agree to Maharaj-ji's plan, but they also said that they didn't want any rent. They were speaking to Maharaj-ji as if they were under some spell. They just kept saying yes. But I was not surprised because if you have been in his presence, then you must know that you can't really say no to him. We had no plans of showing or allotting the cave to anybody, or to take him to the new location, or source those provisions. But when he asks for something, only one word comes out of you: yes.

The next morning, I got a call from Pradeep Brahmachari who had been informed by his kin. He was already near Rishikesh. I gave him our address and he took the next available bus. Vinod and I went to the market to get provisions for Maharaj-ji. It was decided that the next day, Pradeep and I would travel to Gopeshwar, buy the remaining groceries and then go to the new hut at Doghra, while Vinod and Maharaj-ji would leave from our house to get there. Pradeep and Maharaj-ji would stay back and Vinod and I would return home.

That evening was going to be his last meal at our home for a long time. I was feeling very low and depressed. In this short span of time, he had become my anchor, my saviour.

My parents and I were sitting with him in the evening when my mother asked, 'Maharaj-ji, do you think someone has put a curse on us?'

'Why do you think that?'

'Nothing is working out for us.'

'I'm going to tell you something very seriously, so pay attention,' he said. 'You've lost a young one, a family member who took her own life. And after that, you have been to every tantric and every pandit and did whatever they told you to do. Did those things help?'

My mother broke into tears and I had goosebumps. We had never mentioned that my youngest sister had committed suicide. In the heat of an argument with my elder brother, she had picked up and drunk a bottle of pesticide that was used to protect our cauliflower crop. She was dead within 30 minutes. No one could save her and somehow, all of us felt responsible for her death.

'Someone asked you to give a gold chain; another one, a ring. You also sacrificed a goat, kept fasts, did havans—you did everything that they asked you to do, but did those things fix anything?'

She shook her head.

'So have faith in Mother Divine and just do the right thing.'

My father said he was very stressed because the annual fair was exactly 36 days away. With the way it was raining, there was no way that any progress was possible. Forget 36 days, we didn't even hope to complete it in 36 weeks. I felt like punching and kicking myself because it was my stubbornness that led us to be in this position. It was my ambition that had thrust the whole family where we were today: penniless, hopeless and clueless.

At the construction site, even after pouring the concrete, a minimum of 21 days is needed for it settle down. The property had slanted roofs, so curing them with water was another challenge as special arrangements were required to make that happen. That left the flooring, walls, doors, windows and paint work. The meshwork for the roof would take at least 15 days. The labour was on site, but due to incessant rains, they could not do any work.

'Listen, Panditji,' he said to my father, 'you have lovingly fed me for so many days. I will take care of it. For the next 12 days, it will not rain, so complete all the groundwork in 10 days. And then, get the concrete poured onto the roof. Twelve days from now, it will rain every night and be sunny during the day. So your roof will receive its water curing every night, and your work will continue during the day. No power in the three worlds can stop the work from getting completed before the fair. I have eaten food cooked at your home, so I give you my word. It's not something I've done for anyone ever before and it's probably going to be the last time. So sleep with peace.'

He told us to take the support off from the newly built roof after just nine days so that we could complete the flooring, walls and paint work. As I mentioned earlier, normally, after roofing is done, the support is left in place for a minimum of three weeks so that the concrete can set firmly. He said we had his personal guarantee that nothing would happen to the roof, and that this was the only way to save 11 days and complete the project on time. It was unheard of. It was like delivering a healthy baby in the third month of pregnancy.

To say that we sat there shell-shocked would be a gross understatement. He raised his hand in the air and said, 'I do not give anyone my word unless I know I can fulfil it. You can consider it done. Sleep like a baby.'

It has been 10 years since that episode and the roof of the temple is standing strong as ever. The work got completed, the fair went well, we got a bulk of our payment and we paid off our debts. My parents visited Maharaj-ji in Doghra when he was in-between his two sadhanas, to pay their respects. How could they not? For the impossible had happened.

Every night after 12 days, it rained, and every night we sat up and cried and prayed to Maharaj-ji. We bowed in the direction of his hut. We knew he sat there in intense penance and he had made good on his word. Even now, as I pen down these words, my heart is full of gratitude and my eyes are full of tears.

Such is the power of worldly maya, the challenges of the world, that even after knowing who he is and what he is capable of, I have not left everything behind and just joined him in his service.

There are countless such tales of his kindness and humour. He never made me feel any less, in any way, whether it was my education or my circumstances; he always treated me with the utmost respect. A saint with his powers could easily have had me sit in front of him with hands tied, hands folded, head bowed, but not him. He was always so gentle and soft-spoken, it was hard to believe that I had actually met someone like him. When I was growing up, my father would recount stories he had heard from his forefathers—of great sages and their tapas (austere meditation) with which they granted boons to the devotee, while they made their pilgrimage to Uttarakhand. But I had certainly never encountered one in so many years of living in that region.

I had tried to do my best to find Maharaj-ji the most secluded spot for his sadhana. The entire area was under the forest department, and soon, an officer in the forest division got wind that I'd made arrangements for a sadhu to stay there. They asked me to fetch Maharaj-ji and evacuate the place right away.

Chuckling, I said, 'Sure, if you can make him abandon his sadhana mid-way, then you are welcome to try your luck.'

'I'm going to get your Maharaj out in no time and throw his stuff out if he refuses to move,' the officer said. 'He could be poaching tigers or smuggling rare Himalayan herbs for all I know.'

'You can meet him and decide for yourself,' I said to

him. It hurt to hear these words about him from a nobody.

One time, after a sadhana of his ended and before he could commence with his main sadhana, he went down to get some money from the ATM in Gopeshwar. Vinod and I met him in the village and together we hopped into a shared taxi. Half the village had come to seek his blessings. It was such a joyous day. We went to Maharaj-ji's favourite sweet shop in Gopeshwar where they also served samosas without onion and garlic, as per his preference. He would never let us pay and today was no different.

Now call it sheer coincidence, but on our way back in our shared taxi, there sat the forest ranger. I gestured to Maharaj-ji that this was the man who had been enquiring about him. And at that moment, seeing me with a sadhu, he must have guessed the identity of Maharaj-ji as well. The ranger said to him, 'Are you the same Maharaj who is sitting in Doghra?'

'Yes, why?'

'You can't camp or stay there. It's a reserved sanctuary.'

'I'm just quietly doing my sadhana and I'll leave as soon as I am done with my sankalpa (intention set during meditation). In the first week of June.'

'You should have sought permission from the district magistrate (DM) first,' he insisted.

'Listen carefully,' Maharaj-ji said to him, 'I'm a sadhu and I only seek permission from God.'

'The DM will have you removed for sure.'

'If anyone has any power to remove me, they can try. You can convey this to the DM.'

No one spoke for the next few minutes. Vinod and I were feeling elated at seeing the ranger's rear kicked.

'What is your name?' he said to Maharaj-ji.

'My name can be anything. But yours is Prithvi Singh, right?'

He instantly touched his top pocket to see if his name tag was there. It wasn't. He couldn't contain his shock.

'Prithvi means Earth, right?' Maharaj-ji continued. 'Your name is Prithvi Singh and you won't let me be here, on this Prithvi,' said Maharaj-ji with a smile. After this, the ranger did not utter a word. He touched Maharaj-ji's feet when we got down from the taxi.

Maharaj-ji is a yogi, of that there was no doubt in my mind. It felt as if he had stepped out of one of my forefather's stories to straighten my mess. His blessings continued to enrich my life. At the annual fair, the girl who had called me on my phone, came with her parents. Hers was a well-educated family and she had been brought up in Delhi. Would you go and live with a man in a hut made from clay and mud, with a thatched roof, away from civilization? Well, she said she wanted to marry me. Her parents met mine. Initially, no one had been privy to the challenges of this match, but I think, somewhere, this only happened because Maharaj-ji had uttered those words. My marriage was fixed. We had to travel to Delhi.

The government still owed us 20 per cent of the project value, which they said would only be paid after satisfactorily observing the construction for three months after its completion.

With my marriage fixed, I looked in the direction of Maharaj-ji's hut and said, 'You have arranged my marriage but how do I fill the shortage of funds? The government is yet to make the remaining payment for the project.'

By now, I knew well enough that you don't have to tell

him anything or wait for his words. All you have to do is just have faith and then leave it to his will. We pleaded with the department and they released some more funds, just enough to cover our costs.

I left for Delhi with his blessings, my family, the baraatis (groom's wedding procession) and other guests. The wedding went well. On the way back though, I realized that we had spent more than we had expected. I was short of funds. I had forgotten my other ATM card at home and the debit card I had in my wallet had insufficient money. I had all the ATM receipts for the money drawn over the last four days, as I needed to calculate later the expenses that had been made for the wedding. With each withdrawal, my funds had depleted. With a balance of ₹5,000, how was I going to get the bride and the baraatis home?

We had hired four big cars to take us from Mandal to Delhi and back. The distance was 600 kilometres, with a major portion of it made up of difficult terrain and winding roads. The entire cost was roughly coming to ₹30,000. A shortage of ₹25,000 wasn't something I could manage at that point. I requested my Bua (aunt), who was travelling with us, to lend me the money and said that I would return it once we got back home. She agreed to hand over the money the same afternoon, but then she didn't.

In the meantime, I went to the ATM to withdraw my remaining balance. What happened next, knocked the wind out of me. I was so dumbfounded, I sat outside the ATM and cried. I was stumped to find an additional ₹25,000 in my account. I quickly pulled out the last withdrawal receipt from my wallet and it clearly showed a balance of ₹5,000. Then where had this money come from? In disbelief, I withdrew the entire amount. Once outside, I called my father to ask if he had received a message on his phone about a deposit of ₹25,000. He replied that he had received no such notification on his phone. Even if an accidental credit had been made in my account by someone, it could have been any amount! But it was the exact amount that I needed to settle my dues. After the wedding festivities had died down, I discussed the mysterious money deposit in my account with my mother and she asked me the same question—how was it that exact amount? And I said to her, 'I've a feeling that it has something to do with the Maharaj-ji doing his sadhana in Doghra.'

Through the man who would deliver milk to Pradeep Brahmachari, I found out that Maharaj-ji would be going into extreme solitude soon. He would not meet or see anybody during that period. So, if I wanted, I only had three days to go and see him at 12.30 p.m. Maharaj-ji sat in tapasya all day and night. He would only open his hut's door at 12 p.m. to go to Pradeep's hut and have his meal. After that, he would return to his hut and sit in meditation again. No electricity, no running water, no phone, nothing. Just Maharaj-ji in his universe.

I rushed the very next day, and my parched soul was flooded with joy upon seeing him. I sought his blessings, and the first thing that he said to me was, 'I hope there was no shortage of cash and all the expenses were met.'

'But how did you do it, Maharaj-ji? This is beyond me. You couldn't have known my account number! And how could you know how much money I needed?'

He smiled and said, 'Everything went well. There's nothing more to know.'

Pradeep had cooked basmati rice and dal for me. I remember buying that rice only for Maharaj-ji and was surprised to see that he had made the same for him and I.

Brahmachari Pradeep served me a meal alongside Maharaj-ji. The three of us had eaten, but there was still one plate of rice left. I said to Maharaj-ji, 'This is expensive rice. Why waste it? I shall take it along with me and eat it back home.'

He simply smiled and asked Brahmachariji to pack it in a polybag. On my way down, I met a few Nepalis and handed the rice to them. Five months later when I visited Maharaj-ji again, the first thing he said to me was, 'Babloo you didn't get to eat the rice, did you? Those labourers you met on the way had it, right?'

I managed to cover my disbelief with a sheepish smile. Maharaj-ji spoke very little, but when he did, it was always something profound.

A few days after my visit to Maharaj-ji, the same ranger, Prithvi Singh, went to see him in the woods. He was there on a beat and had decided to seek the saint's blessings. He was a changed Prithvi Singh, and he himself recounted the entire experience to me. He even folded his hands while talking about Maharaj-ji.

'Why did you not warn me before, Babloo? He is no ordinary sadhu, or renunciate. He is a siddha purusha (enlightened soul).

'What makes you think that?'

Prithvi Singh told me that his only son had been born with just one testicle. This worried him because he didn't know if his son could be a father one day. So when he met Maharaj-ji, he had voiced his concerns over the preservation of his lineage. '*Mera vansh aage nahin barh sakta.*' (My bloodline will not go any further and will die out with me.)

'That's a load of rubbish,' Maharaj-ji said. 'I don't see any problem. You already have a son, so your lineage is extending.'

Prithvi Singh had wanted to clasp his feet but he was sitting cross-legged. He then told Maharj-ji that it was true that he had a son but he was referring to his son's marriage. Maharaj-ji scolded him and told him to not worry about pointless things. His son was only seven years old at the time. Maharaj-ji said that everything would be fine.

In just one meeting, Prithvi Singh had gone from sarcastically speaking about him, to becoming a life-long devotee of Maharaj-ji.

It was the same effect Maharaj-ji had on anyone he came in contact with. News of a siddha yogi who had come and settled in the woods spread like wildfire. His intense tapasya in the woods in the freezing weather went on for months. It was no longer possible to have his darshan as he sat in dhyana the whole day. Sometimes, it would snow for days and the path to the Anasuya temple would be inaccessible. Many a times, I wondered how Maharaj-ji was meditating on the Divine in that rundown hut. No one could possibly call out to God in that abandoned stable, let alone live there. However, we have since then marked that place as Maharaj-ji's kutir (hut). It's a sacred space for us, made divine by his penance.

Little more than six months later, we heard that Maharaj-ji had received Mother Divine's darshan and there was to be a Kanya-bhoj or Kanchka puja, the holy ritual of feeding and worshipping nine young girls as the nine forms of the Mother Goddess. Seeing him serve the girls prasadam was no ordinary moment. It looked as if he wasn't alone; there seemed a force, a presence with him, surrounding him, emanating from him. There must have been at least 40 or 50 people and they were all starving after that trek. Only after reaching the hut did it occur to us that there were practically no provisions there. Pradeep Brahmachari had already left a day ago.

'Eat to your heart's content,' Maharaj-ji said, 'no one will go hungry.'

If you ever wanted to see a miracle, you should have been there. What seemed like barely enough food for five people, fed everyone in the party and many of us even took double servings.

The owner of Maharaj-ji's hut, and Bhupal Singh, the owner of Pradeep's hut, both reiterated that they did not want any rent. Maharaj-ji made a generous donation for the small temple there to help with its renovation and upkeep. Bhupal Singh went inside the hut with his wife and said that his elder daughter-in-law had three daughters and their younger one had two daughters. Their only wish before they died was to have at least one grandson. I was sitting right there in that hut.

'You've come a bit too late,' Maharaj-ji said. 'Your daughter-in-law is already expecting.' They looked at each other and then at me.

'Please give her your blessings. Anything is possible with it.'

'You had given shelter to Brahmachariji, who was in my service, so I'm indebted to you. Maybe, it's time for me to pay it back.'

Maharaj-ji picked up some ash from his yajna kunda and gave it to the old couple. 'Give it your daughter-in-law. She has to put a pinch of it every day in her food for the next 40 days. Leave the rest to me.'

That is all he said.

Bhupal Singh's daughter-in-law would later give birth to a healthy baby boy, by the way.

Maharaj-ji had always felt special to me, but that day was something else, seeing him emerge from his hut after so many months, his eyes glowing as if alight with fire. As he chanted the mantras, a stillness had settled in the air. He had barely eaten a proper meal for the past few months and yet, he looked powerful and muscled, as if he was returning from a pilgrimage. But pilgrimage to where? In that damp stable that leaked and had no proper roof or a bed? That was out of the question. We took his bag and marched our way to Anasuya temple. Maharaj-ji kept falling in samadhi on the way and he would ask to just sit down at any place. His eyes would go red and then suddenly, within a couple of minutes, they would be white and okay again. He would trek for 30 minutes and again, his eyes would go red and then they would be okay. It was such a striking phenomenon that none of us could ignore it. I wanted to take a picture of him but ever since I had met him, he had shown an aversion to getting photographed.

As soon as we reached the temple, he told me that he had to go to the cave of Atri Muni. On our way, I had showed him a large structure where another sadhu was living. Six months earlier, he had met Maharaj-ji who had given him his word that he would come meet him upon the completion of his sadhana. So when Maharaj-ji sat down in the sadhu's cave, I insisted that I wanted to take a picture for my records. It was my good fortune that he agreed, and so I took a photo with my basic old mobile phone.

Everyone in my family was overjoyed to see Maharaj-ji. My sister came with her son, and my brother also came from Mumbai to seek Maharaj-ji's darshan. No one thought that he would actually stay in the temple for two whole days and give us the seva (service) of serving him meals. I had, however, extracted a promise out of him before he left for his sadhana that he would come and stay with us once it finished, and he made good of his word. He always does. Maharaj-ji planned to leave for his next stint of solitude; anyone could see that he was struggling to be amongst people. He was there, but also wasn't. I had planned that I would not let him go for at least one week, but when I met him two days ago, I figured I must not push him and just let him be.

I shared with Maharaj-ji the details of an astounding tantric, whom my family had been visiting for the last many years. He could just look at you and tell you what was wrong. This tantric would only meet people two days in a week, and every week he spent three nights in the cremation grounds.

'Maharaj-ji,' I asked, 'does he really know or is he simply guessing?'

'It could be either or a combination of those things.'

Maharaj-ji asked me to take him to the tantric. I was puzzled by his request, for he was himself a mahayogi with the Divine vision. Why did he need to go see this man? By sheer coincidence, the next day was the tantric's chosen day for seeing people.

'Babloo,' Maharaj-ji said. 'he's waiting for me.'

And so the next day, we hopped into a shared taxi at Mandal, and then took another one from Gopeshwar to Chamoli. From Chamoli, we took a bus and were about one-third into the journey, when we got off the bus.

We walked a few hundred metres to reach our destination. Next to the river in a decrepit room, sat the tantric. Outside the room, there were tens of pairs of slippers. The room was completely crammed with people. The tantric sat on a raised wooden platform. He was a short dark man with a pronounced squint. In front of him was a pile of cash and fruits. Anyone who visited him would bring an offering of cash, fruits, etc. He was constantly smoking a bidi, and in between drags, he would glance at his hands. The moment Maharaj-ji reached and stood at the door, he took one look at his divine countenance and momentarily stopped talking. He resumed his conversation but continued to steal glances at him. Maharaj-ji told me that he wished to sit by the riverside for a wee bit. It was Ma Ganga, after all, he said.

A few minutes later, Maharaj-ji said that it was time to go in. As soon as he entered the room, the tantric immediately told people to make way. He motioned Maharaj-ji to sit close to him, pointing at a seat made from a blanket. He remained seated, bowed deeply and kept his hands folded for some time. Maharaj-ji told him to continue and not stop on his account.

Next, a couple approached the tantric and when they narrated their problem, he looked at Maharaj-ji and said to the couple, 'How can I say anything? My tantra-mantra and totka will fail completely in his presence. The saint you see here is not just a saint, he is an incarnation, someone who comes once in a yuga. Just take his blessings and leave.' And then he instructed everyone in the room to take Maharaj-ji's blessings instead and leave. He announced that he was done for the day and asked Maharaj-ji if he could sit in his presence for just a couple of minutes.

Maharaj-ji started singing a beautiful eulogy to the Goddess. I couldn't understand anything as it was in Sanskrit, but it sounded so melodious and powerful, I thought my ears would melt away. As Maharaj-ji sang, the tantric began crying profusely. As soon as the divine eulogy finished, it was as if everything had merged into Maharaj-ji.

'Maharaj-ji, I'm going to die like a dog,' he lamented, 'Not at home in peace, not even in my son's arms; they won't even find the pieces of my body.'

'That's true. That fate awaits you.' Maharaj-ji acknowledged.

'Please help me, Maharaj-ji,' he said, as he bowed down and caught his feet and started to cry.

I sat there wondering what was going on—the famous tantric of our region was begging Maharaj-ji for help. The next moment, he kept his hand on the tantric's head and whispered, 'Henceforth, you are free of your past karma and will die in peace.'

He then said to the tantric that, from now on, he mustn't abuse the gift Mother Divine had given him. He must tell people only that which Mother whispers in his ear and not add 10 things of his own to make more money and fool people. The tantric cried even harder as unabated tears of gratitude poured from his eyes.

He bent down again, and with his two hands took all the cash in front of him and offered it all to Maharaj-ji.

Maharaj-ji turned it down, but the tantric persisted. He got up to leave as he really didn't want to take anything. I told the tantric that I'd never seen Maharaj-ji take anything, certainly never any cash. But the man was adamant and he ran out after Maharaj-ji with the tributes. 'Please redeem me and accept my humble offering. In the last 20 years, this is the first time I have gotten up from my seat without my closing prayer. You mean everything to me. I know who you are. Please take it.'

'Consider that I've accepted, and now you have it back as my blessing.'

Just then, we noticed that there were quite a few people outside. They fell at Maharaj-ji's feet. The people had come a few minutes ago but could not gather the courage to enter the room. They said the chanting they heard had rooted them to the ground and they had stood there spellbound.

On our way back, referring to the tantric, Maharaj-ji said to me that the man would have been hit by a speeding truck, his body parts flung in different directions. They would have found it difficult to sew him back together. Nothing was hidden from Maharaj-ji, I thought. But in his presence, the enormity of his prowess was something I kept forgetting because sometimes, he would tease me like a younger brother.

As we walked back to the main road, we came across a small tailor shop. It was practically in the middle of nowhere. Maharaj-ji walks very fast and I was trying to keep up with him. Seeing the shop, he slowed down a bit. The man behind the counter was staring at him, transfixed. Maharaj-ji had initially passed the shop but then told me that he wanted to visit it.

'That man needs to see me,' he said looking at me.

'Oh Maharaj-ji, it's your radiance that makes people stare

at you. Ignore him. What can the tailor possibly have to say to you?'

But Maharaj-ji insisted that I call him. The tailor came forward and bent to touch his feet. Maharaj-ji said to him, 'Your son is unwell. He's in the hospital.' The tailor's eyes welled up and he pleaded with him to do something.

Smiling gently, Maharaj-ji said to the tailor, 'Go now, he'll be fine. You've nothing to worry about. He'll be discharged before tomorrow's sunset.'

We walked to the bus stop and Maharaj-ji ordered me to return home. I wanted to accompany him to Rishikesh but he said that he didn't want to waste my time.

A few years later, my mother fell sick and was diagnosed with cancer. We took her to the hospital for her tests. Her chemotherapy and radiation started, and she suffered every day. I missed Maharaj-ji so much. I managed to get in touch with his PA who immediately got back to me.

'Please cure my mother or take her to your loka, Maharaj-ji.' I conveyed my message through the PA.

'It's time for her to go,' Maharaj-ji conveyed. 'Say Om Swami and blow into her ears.'

On the third day, she was gone.

I am busy with my family and livelihood, working hard to put food on the table and pay my bills, but not a day goes by when I don't think of Maharaj-ji.

There are many people who ask about him in our town. They remember him like he was here yesterday. He has touched many lives. Even though Maharaj-ji hasn't visited us in many years, the tailor still asks about him every time he sees me. I remember and revere him in my heart, and I hope you too get to witness the glory and grace of my Maharaj-ji someday.

I am so glad that a Hindi translation of his memoir fell into my lap. Otherwise, I'd have never known that Maharaj-ji has not made any mention of his powers and kindness in the book. As I mentioned earlier, I was not happy but in fact angry after reading that memoir. Why did he falsely give the impression that he was just an ordinary being? All he had to do was tell the complete truth and include at least some of the numerous miracles he has performed over the years. I felt so helpless, even let down. That very day I had decided that one day I would write a book on Maharaj-ji. And had I not met Sadhvi Vrindaji in the ashram, I would not have gotten this opportunity to set the record straight. I am so thankful to her.

If you see Maharaj-ji talk lovingly and casually, please don't mistake him for an ordinary mortal. Believe me, he is not. I have observed him from close quarters. Don't fall into his trap of 'simplicity,' otherwise you will lose out on a lot. Look at the facts of his life and look past his so-called simple talk. He's a *chaliya* (trickster) like Vishnu. Don't let him hide from you. Let him reveal himself to you. That is my prayer for each one of us.

Lifeline

Pooja Sharma

Swamiji has been an important part of my life since the day I got married to Rajan, my amazing husband and Swamiji's elder brother, in 2002.

'There is only thing I ask of you,' Rajan had said to me before our marriage. 'Amit is dearer to me than anyone in my life. I cannot imagine my life without him, so wherever we stay, we'll always stay together. He'll stay with us. I will give you everything you want, I will provide for you in every way imaginable, but please always take care of my little brother.'

I do not like to refer to Swamiji by his old name, so please allow me to continue addressing him as Swamiji even when he was known as Amit Sharma.

When Rajan asked me for that promise, I didn't think much of it. In fact, I didn't find it odd that before marrying me he was telling me that someone other than me was dearer to him. And there's a good reason for that. Over our courtship, which lasted about three years, I had heard so much about Swamiji that I was curious to know more about him. Somewhere in my mind, even though I didn't doubt what was said of him, I did feel that perhaps it was all a bit exaggerated.

Imagine for a moment someone telling you that there is a 20-year-old man that people have been revering over a decade because he chants the Vedas like the back of his hand or that he makes accurate predictions with astrology. Or that he is a computer whiz-kid. He plays the keyboard, he plays chess and is a rated player. Furthermore, he was an editor of a newspaper at age 16 and had already been published in many American journals and magazines. That, at age 20, he was a deeply religious person, a teetotaller, a vegetarian and someone who had never been to a dance club even though he was living abroad. I was born in a Sikh family and these concepts of diet and restraint were alien to me. We believed in living life to the fullest: we worked hard and partied hard.

Getting back to Swamiji, I was told that here was a 20-year-old who spoke Sanskrit as fluently as English and that he had a hypnotic effect on people. Someone who was winning tournaments in badminton and had breezed through his three-year degree in one and a half years in Sydney. That a 20-year-old had a hand in building Australia's first multi-currency payment system with encryption and other crazy sounding technical terms. That he meditated and did his sadhanas every day without fail. I was told that when he was 17, he had already finished the coursework of chartered accountancy because those fat books had sat in Rajan's bookshelf—Swamiji had devoured them in no time. This young guy had been investing in stocks and writing columns from the age of 15. Oh, and did I mention, at 20, he was earning a quarter of a million dollars and driving a convertible. All this while he was still on a student visa in

Australia. Remember, we are talking about a person who was born in a small town with very limited access to resources. The internet did not even exist back then.

Please spare a thought for me for a moment. What would you think if someone told you all of the above, and much more, was about just one person, barely out of his teens? What had happened? Was he a superman or were people out of their minds? At times, I wanted Rajan to talk about me, about us, but his favourite and most passionate topic was his little brother. So much so, he told me that he wouldn't marry me unless I had Swamiji's nod. But the strange thing was, barring a few moments here and there, I never felt jealous or felt that Swamiji had almost entirely taken up all the space in Rajan's heart and mind. I don't know why, but my own heart and mind never revolted.

Today, I feel so grateful that Rajan had me make that promise, for we were blessed to spend those years with Swamiji in Sydney and, for a brief period, in Canada, before he renounced his material life. Over the years, I have learnt that every second spent in Swamiji's presence is nothing short of a miracle. It is eternity locked in a moment. The joy of cooking for him and feeding him exceeds any other. And I say that as a mother. It's not that I cared for him because I gave Rajan the promise, it's just that from the moment I met him, he commanded such respect and love. If God ever granted you the chance to be in his company, you will know exactly what I mean.

I was in my early 20s when I first met Swamiji. My earliest memories of him are that of an extremely kind and loving person, dressed impeccably in designer clothes, handmade

Italian shoes and extravagantly expensive watches. Nothing flashy and everything classy. In his minimalist look was great opulence, if I may put it that way. Swamiji was visiting India in December 2000. Rajan and I wouldn't get married until February 2002. In fact, during this particular visit, Rajan was already in Sydney. He asked me to meet Swamiji and spoke to me all night about his wonderful, prodigious brother.

On the day of the meeting, I was nervous and my heart was pounding. I took my father's car and drove to Swamiji's home. I was scared to meet someone so sharp and intelligent. What if he asked me about things I didn't know? What if I made a fool of myself? What if he spoke to me in Sanskrit? What if he didn't approve of me? What if he asked me to cook a meal? Other than making an omelette, I knew absolutely nothing else. 'What if, what if, what if,' my head was exploding. *'Oh God, Rajan, why aren't you here?'* I thought.

The plan was that I would take Swamiji out for lunch and then drive him back home. Rajan, however, had told me to be prepared for anything. That Swamiji might change any plan at any moment and say that he would like to eat at home instead or might not eat at all. As if I wasn't nervous enough...

I parked my car outside their home and knocked on the door. Swamiji came out. He gave a wide smile and my nervousness reappeared in an instant. I started bumbling and rambling right in front of him. He heard me patiently for a little while and then said, 'Should we go inside?'

I apologized and immediately made my way inside. He was dressed in casuals. Nike track pants, t-shirt, watch and a phone. That's all he had on him. A very unassuming, simple, down-to-earth person. But have you ever seen a high-ranking officer in the defence forces or a bureaucrat? Even at home, there's something about them that gives away their stature. Swamiji was no different; there was great politeness but no casualness about him. Even in those clothes, it felt like he owned the whole town.

He asked me how I was and brought me a glass of water. His gentle manner immediately put me at ease. Now, the most important part: remember Rajan, my would-be husband, and our elaborate plans of taking Swamiji out for lunch? Well, it turned out that he had forgotten to inform his little brother. So Swamiji had no clue. He thought I had just come to meet with him. And there I was, having made two trips to the restaurant already—I had booked a table, instructed and even tipped the people there to ensure immaculate service. Of course, I couldn't and didn't say all this to Swamiji. Rajan! I was grinding my teeth.

We continued to talk and then Swamiji asked me if I would like to have a cup of tea. Even then, I couldn't dare to tell him that I had booked a table and that we were supposed to eat out. Instead, I offered that I would love to make tea for him. He was a little surprised, but agreed. There was only one problem. I had never made tea in my life. I didn't even drink tea. I drank cola and coffee. Like I said, I *only* knew how to make an omelette. I don't even know why I used the word 'tea'. We went to the kitchen and he showed me where everything was. Just then his phone rang, and he walked out of the kitchen to take the call. I loved his accent from the very first time I heard it.

Thankfully, making tea is no rocket science. I figured, put tea leaves, sugar, milk and water in one go and boil. That's what I did. I filtered and poured it in two cups. I was so happy that I could make tea. I couldn't find any cookies and the like to serve, but that was all right, I thought. He finished his work call and told me that he was planning to start his own company and had been chasing this potential customer for quite some time now.

He sipped the tea and I asked him if it was all right. He spoke so highly of my tea that I thought I was the best tea maker in the world. I was over the moon. In my excitement and to show how intelligent I was, I told him that it was the first time I had ever made tea. He reminded me that my tea was cold and that I should drink it too. 'Of course,' I said. 'You finish yours, too, and if you want I'll make another cup for you.' He thanked me and said it wouldn't be necessary. 'Just this one delightful cup is enough for the entire day.'

With great finesse, I picked up the cup and took the first sip. The next moment, I was looking for a place to spit it all out.

'I'm so sorry,' I said. 'Oh God, I'm so sorry. I think I accidentally put salt in it.'

Swamiji laughed heartily, and with each moment I was getting more embarrassed. He told me to not worry, then went in the kitchen and came out with two cups of tea. It was the first time I had tea, and even today I remember its taste. It was sweet, pun intended.

Seeing how easy it was to talk to him, I finally told him that we had planned to eat lunch outside. He grabbed his wallet, put on his sports shoes and said he was ready to go. I thought he would dress up, but he looked just as immaculate in anything. We went out and he opened the door for me.

For the record, it was the first time anyone had shown me such chivalry. Once in the car, he apologized saying he wasn't comfortable driving a car in India, so if I could drive, he'd appreciate it. 'My mind will adjust in a few days' time and then I'll be fine driving here. But since it's not my car, I don't want to take any chances,' he said.

We had a wonderful lunch, and all I remember is that, for the most part, I laughed and laughed. The funniest person I've known in my life is Rajan. He can make comedy out of the most serious situations. And Swamiji proved that they were brothers, after all. He too, was very funny. Once they pick a point, these two will continue to make you laugh until your tummy hurts.

At no point did Swamiji try to show off his intelligence and accomplishments or talk down to me. I remember thinking he should have been *my* little brother. Everything just felt right around him.

I was blessed to be under the protection of this divine soul. Truthfully though, I realized this much later in life. Just as we find it hard to fathom the deepest parts of the ocean, till date, I have been unable to fathom him. Each year new incidents and events unfold, subsequently strengthening my faith and belief in him.

He didn't let me pay at lunch. I still remember, at first, the staff refused to take the bill from me as I had already tipped them. Swamiji asked the waiter how much I had given him in gratuity. He just continued to smile and kept his head low. The bill was some 270 rupees or so.

'I'll give you a thousand rupees in tip,' Swamiji said to him. 'Let me pay.'

The guy immediately handed the check to Swamiji and put my 50-rupee note on that table and said, 'Sorry, Madam. Can't take from you.'

Swamiji threw back his head and laughed. 'I'm very happy with you,' he said to the waiter, and handed him three crisp 500-rupee notes. 'Keep the rest.'

Later, I would discover on countless occasions that when it came to money, Swamiji spent it like he didn't need it. His money worked for him, served him. In my 21 years of knowing him, he has not once shown any attachment to money. 'Tipping gives me the opportunity to reward someone. It's my chance to do some good and it gives me a lot of joy,' he would say. I have routinely seen him tip $50, $100 and, on occasions, even $500. 'I try to make it memorable for the server,' he would say.

Rajan called me that night and said Swamiji loved me. 'She's the best partner you can ever have. She's a beautiful soul and a very genuine person. So, as far as I'm concerned, it's truly a match made in heaven,' he told Rajan. From that moment, Rajan was certain that no one could stop us from getting married. But why would anyone stop us, you might wonder?

Well, I belonged to a Sikh family and Rajan was born into a Hindu one. Not only were they Hindus, but they were religious Brahmins. In our family, all relatives had to be consulted before marrying off a boy or girl. So neither my parents nor any of my relatives approved of my relationship with Rajan. I had never even been to a temple but only Gurudwaras. I knew nothing about their religion. But I was sure of Rajan. He was a competent and strong man. And after meeting Swamiji, I had no doubt that if I ever wanted to be a part of a family, it would be this one.

So I put my foot down, and said I was only going to marry Rajan and no one else. Swamiji had already travelled back to Sydney and he was busy all the time. Rajan and I spoke daily over the phone. He spent thousands of dollars in phone bills because Skype was the only alternative and my dial-up connection was both expensive and useless. So the phone it was. At one point, it felt like my parents would never give me permission to marry Rajan.

One day, he called me and put Swamiji on speaker phone. 'Listen,' Swamiji said, 'have no worries whatsoever. Nothing in the world can stop you two from getting married because it is destiny. Fate has already ordained it.'

'But my parents are strictly against it.'

'Let me know if it's still the case in seven days from now.'

'Why? What will happen in seven days?'

'You'll see for yourself.'

'Please elaborate,' I implored.

'Pooja,' Rajan intervened. 'If he has said we'll get married, we will. There are no two ways about it. If he has said something will happen in seven days, it will. Don't ask him to elaborate. Just let his words unfold.'

The situation at home was incredibly tense. Everyone was trying to talk me out of this relationship. But I was adamant. In fact, I had never been surer about anything else in my life. I stopped talking to my parents and they stopped talking to me. I had turned vegetarian after meeting Rajan, a change that only got amplified after a single meeting with Swamiji. My relatives and parents did not approve of me becoming a vegetarian. Earlier, all three meals used to be non-vegetarian and now I wasn't even eating cakes that contained egg. It was a huge culture shock to my parents and extended family.

My parents had been incredibly loving people all their lives. I was the apple of their eyes. It was just my sister and I, and our parents had brought us up like boys. Since I was the younger one, I was allowed many more liberties. I would even sip whisky from my father's drink and he never stopped me. It hurt me deeply to see them in pain, but I was confused and lost. Despite their love for me, they would not let me marry Rajan. It wasn't like Rajan was unemployed or unlettered. He was handsome, intelligent, sweet, funny, caring and had a well-paying job. Was I to reject him just because he was born into a different religion?

Now that Swamiji had said that something would happen in seven days, I waited with bated breath. But what could possibly change? Things were going from bad to worse. I was living like a stranger in my own home. I would lock my room and stay indoors all day. Just like I was sure that this was the right decision, they were sure that it wasn't. It was a stalemate.

And then on the fifth day, there was a knock on our door. None of us were in a condition to meet anyone. But, oh my God, there stood Pitashree, Rajan and Swamiji's father, ringing the doorbell. It was not just unexpected, it was incomprehensible. If you know anything about Indian culture, you must know that a boy's father (from an older generation) will not make the first move to seek a girl's hand for his son. Particularly when he knows that his son has a ton of other options. I recognized him because I had seen his pictures and even had a chance encounter with him once. My parents, however, had no idea who he was.

He introduced himself and said, 'My son and your daughter want to marry each other, and I don't have any problem about us belonging to different religions. There's only one God, after all.'

My parents were immediately put at ease and they said they needed a bit more time as they had to consult other family members. They mentioned they were a bit apprehensive and unsure about the whole thing.

'It's important to consult all our relatives,' my father said.

'Look at me,' Pitashree said, 'I haven't even consulted my wife before coming here. 'Your relatives are not going to pay their bills, so how does their opinion matter?'

'My son doesn't drink or smoke,' he continued. 'He's a teetotaller. He holds an Australian work visa. My wife and I are government employees. We have no liabilities on our head nor any loans to repay. We are a small, educated and happy family. What else do you want?'

His candid talk blew my parents away. He mentioned that he had been having sleepless nights because he was worried that Rajan and I might do something childish or stupid that we might all regret later. Pitashree is truly a straightforward and humble man. In my nearly 20 years of marriage to Rajan, I have never seen Pitashree boast about anything.

'All I am trying to tell you,' he said, 'is that they are both young and want to marry. Who will be responsible if they took any untoward step? What if your daughter did something to herself or my son to himself? Besides, they are adults in the eyes of the law and are entitled to marry whoever they wish to.'

He had a cup of tea with a cookie, and left. Pitashree's impeccable reasoning left my parents speechless. My father immediately booked his ticket to go to Delhi so he could speak about the matter with my very religious grandfather. We were sure that my paternal grandfather would never approve of this match because he was a staunch Sikh.

When my father narrated the whole saga and my wish to him, my grandfather said, '*O yaar, Manjeet, is vich kehdi vadi gal eh? Je munda changa hai te udha ghar-bar changa hai, teh pher tu kehdi soch vich paya hoya hain? Eh vi babaji di kirpa hai.*' (What's the big deal? If the boy and his family are good people, what are you worried about? This is also God's grace.)

And so, we had my grandfather's blessings, too. On the seventh day, my parents called Pitashree to inform him that they were ready to go ahead with the alliance. Imagine a struggling farmer whose crop had been dying in a drought spanning several years and then suddenly, out of nowhere, it rains and the streams run once again, the fields are green again, his livelihood is restored. Such was the state of my mind. After months, I sat down and had dinner with my parents.

This was my first experience of the subtle forces that hide behind that gentle smile of Swamiji. What I would also learn is that if you push him to give you his word or say yes to something, it's never the same as when he does it of his own accord. Whether you believe in God or not, the thing I can tell you for sure is this: Swamiji is the politest and most gentlemanlike character you'll ever meet in your life.

My roka, a ritual confirming the commitment to marry, was done while Rajan and Swamiji were still in Sydney. It was decided that the marriage would take place on 15 February 2002.

In January, a month and a half prior to the wedding, my mother woke up one morning with an excruciating pain in her lower legs and spine. She couldn't move at all. It all happened so suddenly. We rushed her to the hospital and found out that she had a slipped disc. She was bedridden for a seemingly never-ending time. I bathed her, fed her and looked after her daily hygiene routine for a month. A thought that repeatedly crossed my mind was that who would take care of her once I left for Sydney? My mother would cry and, seeing her plight, I would break down, too. She had always led such an active life. She had much faith in God and prayed as much as she could while lying in bed.

On 3 February, Rajan and Swamiji came to my house for the first time to meet my parents. My mother (her condition not having improved) was very emotional on seeing Rajan, her future son-in-law, for the very first time. She said that she wanted to attend my wedding but would be unable to. Tears started streaming down her face and mine. I couldn't bear to see her like this. And then I saw Swamiji inching close, taking my mother's hand in his, looking into her eyes and saying, 'Aunty, you will come to the wedding and do the kanyadan (Hindu ritual of the bride's parents giving her away at the wedding) with your own hands.'

Back then, looking at her condition, it seemed impossible. When the magical day finally arrived, my mother, with the help of a walking stick and a belt tied around her waist, walked with me to the sacred fire pit. Rajan and I took the seven pheras around the Vedi, the sacred platform set up for weddings and other religious rituals, (as per the Hindu custom) to be together for eternity. This auspicious ceremony was performed by Swamiji himself, along with another panditji. The wedding went off well, and my mother, overcome with emotion and gratitude for Swamiji's blessings, could not hold back her tears. That day marked the beginning of my deep respect and love for Swamiji. Somewhere in my mind, when that first incident about the 'seven days' had happened, I still thought it was Swamiji making a prediction as an astrologer. But when my mother walked with me at the wedding, something shifted in me. It felt like he was not just making predictions but was actively shaping the future.

On our wedding day, Swamiji put the keys of a brand-new car, a Honda Civic, in our hands and gifted us a trip to New Zealand. I had only seen people giving away cars as a present in the movies. It is easy to forget that Swamiji was only 22 at the time.

On the very first day that I entered their home, I was bombarded with gifts from everyone. Pitashree gave me ₹51,000 in shagun (a token of good luck) and said to me very lovingly, 'Beta, should I go and get a picture of Guru Nanak Dev or Guru Gobind Singhji or any other Guruji for you? Shall I fetch the Sukhmani Sahib or any other gutka (a small book containing extracts from the Guru Granth Sahib)? You can put pictures of any guru sahib you want at the altar.' This simple sentence made me break into tears. His loving statement evoked emotions those gifts could not. He brought me a beautiful picture of Guru Nanak Dev.

After my marriage, my Australian visa got denied and I could not accompany Rajan as he boarded the return flight to Sydney on 27 February 2002. I was in tears. Matarani, Pitashree, Didi and Suvi Bhaiya all tried to comfort me, but the thought of not being with my dear husband broke my spirit. After Rajan left, I moved back to my parents' house to look after my mother. She, however, had become quite independent in her daily chores. She only needed to tie a belt around her waist and move about slowly. Swamiji's blessing had put her back on her feet for good.

Just two days later, on 1 March, Rajan and Swamiji advised me to once again go to Delhi and get my medical examination done for the Australian visa. Swamiji asked me to call him when I reached the embassy. Once I was there, he told me not to worry and that I would be in Sydney by 10 March.

When my anxiety and fear did not subside, he said, 'PB, if you are not having dinner with us in Sydney on 10 March, I'll never make a prediction again. You have my word. Your visa, ticket, flight, everything will go smoothly.'

I was humbled and completely knocked off my feet. This time, I did get my visa and reached Sydney on the exact date foretold by Swamiji.

I was incredibly fortunate that I met Rajan and through him became part of such a loving and generous family. They are my rock and my comfort. Few people have such a privilege.

As soon as I reached home, I saw the gift-wrapped car in the garage. Rajan hadn't opened it yet because he had been waiting for me. Swamiji's black convertible Saab was parked outside. 'Your haughty Honda has kicked my black beauty out,' Swamiji joked.

The next day, I woke up to the sound of chanting in a deep, unearthly voice. At first I was intimidated, and then, intrigued. This was a beautiful three-bedroom house. We had the master bedroom with a huge walk-in wardrobe. Swamiji had the other bedroom where he also had his study table, and the third one was set up as a pooja room, which had a small altar. I had heard him chant on the day of our marriage as well, but I had been so preoccupied and dazed that day that nothing had registered. Today, however, something was different.

Over the next few months, I came to know that every morning, Swamiji meditated and then chanted the Rudram, followed by the Shiva panchakshara stotra, in a loud voice. The entire home would reverberate with his chanting. If you have ever heard Swamiji chant the Vedic mantras then you must know that he recites the Vedas in a very deep voice.

His voice was so loud and clear that it reached a deep octave. The walls of the house, and all the living and non-living things rejoiced in his beautiful and melodious singing. I would try to understand what or who he was singing about but would be unsuccessful in my endeavours.

One day, Swamiji read my mind (which happened a lot) and explained the verses of the beautiful eulogy to me. It left a lasting impact on me, as did the many Vedic chants and stutis (prayers) that Swamiji would often sing. I was so attracted to the beautiful chants that at once Lord Shiva made way into my heart, and since then I have never let a day pass without praying to Him in the morning and evening. It was as if an entirely new world had opened up to me.

The fancy suits, expensive watches, his keen business sense, nothing could ever obscure his deep spiritual side. You couldn't miss the calm in his face or the clarity in his eyes. Gentle and loving, he helped anyone who asked him for help.

You might feel that I am endlessly glorifying Swamiji, something he disapproves of openly, but if you could look into my heart, you would know that I want the whole world to experience the joy that his mere thought brings to a genuine seeker. I don't even know where to start, whether it be his polite manners, chivalry, ultra-sharp mind or his immaculate personality.

In fact, I would say of him what Einstein said of Mahatma Gandhi, 'Generations to come will scarce believe that such a one as this ever in flesh and blood walked upon this earth.'

I have always been talkative and can go on and on for hours without a break. I remember I'd bore Swamiji in Sydney with the latest anecdotes and stories, but he always listened patiently, without ever interrupting me, while he continued to work on his laptop. Swamiji worked day and night as he ran his own business. He would occasionally raise his head, make eye contact, smile and ask me to continue with my tales, and then return to his screen. He would always address me as PB, short for Pooja Bhabhi, since he first met me.

In May 2003, Matarani visited us for a few months in Sydney to attend Swamiji's MBA graduation ceremony, scheduled for June. This was her second visit. She had also come for Swamiji's bachelor's graduation ceremony back in 2000. I was lucky to be able to spend some quality time with her as I had immediately come to Sydney after my marriage. I was staying at home, trying to learn how to manage the new place and, above all, enjoying my time with Rajan and Swamiji.

Matarani is so wise, spiritual, loving and forgiving. I learned many things from her, especially letting go of my ego to become a new, better me. She has always guided me like my own mother, and during her visit, she advised me to look for a job and learn to be self-reliant and independent. She told me that for a woman to be financially independent was a feeling like no other. So, once she left for India, I was keen on acting on her wise words. I tried looking for work everywhere, pleading to Swamiji to make my resume, which he so gracefully did. I applied to a few companies but within a few weeks, I lost patience.

I had applied for a lot of jobs and was just getting rejections from everywhere. My confidence was shredded to pieces. I thought I would never get a job.

One evening, Rajan and I were cleaning the kitchen. Swamiji was punching away at his laptop at a distance. Suddenly, I broke into tears and told Rajan that I would never be independent and stand on my own two feet. He stopped cleaning the shelf and hugged me in an attempt to soothe me. I started crying even harder. Swamiji looked up from his screen to observe the scene unfolding in the kitchen. He stopped working and came up to me.

'You really want a job?' he said.

'Yes, that's all I want,' I cried.

'We can increase your pocket money so you won't miss having a job. How about $2,000 per month?'

'No, it's not the same. I just want a job!'

'Are you sure?'

'Yes, that's all I want,' I parroted.

'That's all?' he said. 'Here.'

He took a few drops of water from the kitchen tap that was still running, whispered a mantra and sprinkled it on me in one swift movement.

'Done,' he said. 'I have written the job in your destiny. *Ja kya yaad karegi.*' (Consider it done. You can thank me later!).

The very next morning, my phone rang and I was called in for an interview as a research analyst with Thomson Reuters.

On Wednesday, I appeared for the interview; on Friday they sent me the offer letter and on Monday, I joined the organization. On my first day, while leaving for the office, I burst into tears.

Rajan and Swamiji argued that it was hardly fair. Why was I crying now?

'Now I won't be able to make hot breakfast or lunch for you,' I said.

'PB, it's my good fortune since I was only eating the food you make for your sake. *Ishvar ne tumhari nahin, meri suni hai*,' joked Swamiji. (God has listened to my prayers, not yours.) I burst into laughter.

On the bus to work, I was a little anxious about joining a new company, but the reality of how quickly my wish had become a reality finally dawned on me. I was baffled by his power. He just had to utter the words and every wish could be granted. In my mind, Swamiji had a magic wand and he had the power to fulfil our dreams.

I was excited at my new-found self-reliance; I was making money and becoming independent. The job was great but demanding. I had to wake up extremely early in the morning as my office was in downtown Sydney. By the time I was back home, after Rajan and I cooked dinner, I would be so tired that I would go to sleep by 9 p.m. Looking back, I think I was like a child at a day care who tires herself out after a long day. My workload was immense and I barely spent any time with Swamiji and Rajan. I continued working for a while, grateful to Swamiji for giving me my first job on a platter.

~

> The woods are lovely, dark and deep,
> But I have promises to keep,
> And miles to go before I sleep,
> And miles to go before I sleep.

This is a stanza from the famous poem 'Stopping by Woods on a Snowy Evening' by Robert Frost. It is one of Swamiji's favourites, besides 'I Wandered Lonely as a Cloud' by William Wordsworth and 'A Psalm of Life' by H.W. Longfellow. He loved to read and share with us what he had been reading at the dining table. Every time we went out for a cup of coffee, Swamiji would stop by a bookstore and find at least two or three books to his liking and approach the counter with a big smile on his face. His eyes would sparkle at the sight of books. It was endearing to see him so excited. In all the years that I have spent with him, I have never seen his enthusiasm for either meditation or reading go down. He never compromised on either of these two things. Come rain or shine, he would sit for sadhana at a predetermined time. In those days, Swamiji would also play the keyboard in his spare time.

In 2005, Rajan and I decided to move to Canada with Swamiji. His business was expanding all over the world and especially in the United States of America. It was a better move, we thought. Instead of waiting for months to see him, we would be in immediate proximity to him.

In July 2005, we found out we were expecting our first baby. Swamiji had just come back from Sydney after finishing his project with the New South Wales Police. I was a bit nervous as the baby wasn't planned. I was still adjusting to life in an entirely new country. Swamiji told me to have the baby and not to interfere with nature's gift.

I did an upaya (astrological remedy) for a few days, as suggested by Swamiji. I was so blessed that Rajan and Swamiji took care of me—from driving me to regular doctor appointments and check-ups, taking me to restaurants at odd hours to fulfil my cravings, to listening to all my blabbering and, at times, emotional tantrums as well. They gave me unconditional love and support, making sure that I just rested and listened to soothing bhajans, read good books and exercised at home. A quote by Carrie Fisher quite aptly sums up my state of mind in those days:

'Everything grows rounder and wider and weirder, and I sit here in the middle of it all and wonder who in the world you will turn out to be.'

We requested him to name our baby. He told us if it was a girl, we should name her Ida, and if it was a boy, he would be named Adi. I remember asking him what the two names meant; of course, he was already getting to that before I, as usual, interrupted him with my excitement. Ida meant comfort in Sanskrit and was associated with lunar energy. Adi meant prime, or first, in Sanskrit. Swamiji also mentioned Adi Shankaracharya—the ideal sannyasi and great philosopher.

Whenever Swamiji played the keyboard, somehow, I would get the feeling that there was a big apple inside of me that was rejoicing, kicking and listening to the melodious tunes. The pregnancy progressed smoothly until I was in my last trimester. As it turned out, I was overweight. I was informed that if I went past 166 pounds, I would have to have a C-section.

I came home with Rajan and told Swamiji that I would eat less to watch my weight.

'PB,' Swamiji said in his sweet, assuring tone, 'No C-section will happen. I'm here for you. Eat to your heart's content.'

For the next few weeks, I continued to eat plenty of junk food and visited numerous restaurants. The weighing scale stood still at 165 pounds.

My due date was 24 March 2006. We were old school about it and decided not to find out the gender of the baby. And all of a sudden, Swamiji had to leave for an urgent meeting with Microsoft in Seattle on 27 March. He would return only on 30 March.

'But, Swamiji,' I said. 'I am already overdue. The baby will be out any moment. Your leaving for a meeting in a different country is giving me anxiety.'

'PB,' he said, 'I promise you I will be there for the birth of your son.'

'Son?' I exclaimed.

'Uh...' Swamiji cleared his throat and smiled. 'I mean, baby. At the birth of your baby.'

'If you tell me now,' I said, 'I can buy the clothes accordingly.'

'How do I know?' he shrugged. 'But the sky is quite blue today, isn't it?' And he pointed at the sky. I resumed my crying and told him that I would wait for him. After he left, with tears in my eyes, I pointed my finger at my tummy and said in a stern voice, 'Listen, whoever you are, you cannot come out until Swamiji has returned from his meeting.'

Swamiji had promised he would be there, holding the baby and naming our baby as well. He would then give the baby the first suckle of sweet honey and his sacred blessings. During the next two days, I kept telling the baby to wait, that its time had not yet come. And I kept up with my prayers as well. Like oxygen in the air nourishes the body, faith in Swamiji nourished my heart and soul; it anchored me.

Swamiji arrived on 30 March, a little late in the night, after finishing his business commitments. Finally, on 1 April, on a bright, sunny Saturday morning, Rajan and I went to Trillium Hospital. With Swamiji back in town, I was finally ready. We were there for a check-up to find the specifics of the birth—an approximate time, whether it would happen by inducing labour, etc. But as soon as we arrived, I was admitted. With the baby being eight days overdue and our first newborn as well, the doctors were very careful. I told Rajan to let Swamiji know immediately, and an hour later, around 10 a.m., he arrived to speak to us.

Swamiji put his hand on my head, blessed me and assured me it wouldn't be long now. He said he would wait outside. The ordeal began soon enough. I was clenching Rajan's hand as tight as I could, my nails digging into his skin. At last, we welcomed our firstborn, Adi. His Jatakarma, a ritual done soon after birth, was performed by Swamiji. A mantra was whispered into his ears, and as per the Hindu tradition, a tiny drop of honey (signifying a beautiful life ahead) was placed into his mouth. It was truly an amazing moment.

~

When Adi was nearly two years old, on one of our trips to the Iskcon Temple in Pittsburgh, Swamiji bought a beautiful painting of a little Krishna playing with Ma Yashoda. I was ecstatic when I first saw how mesmerizingly beautiful it was.

I took Adi to the home country in December 2008.

Swamiji had moved back to India by then. One day, Swamiji said that Adi's sibling was in the making. I laughed, saying that Adi already kept me on my toes. But as always, his words came to pass. I was in the family way in the last week of February, and Rajan and I were expecting our second baby by end of November 2009. I happily wondered if, like in Adi's case, this delivery would be overdue as well. Perhaps then, my next child and Swamiji would come to share the same birthday! I gave Swamiji the news on the phone and a few days later, he gave me a mantra to chant.

A few months passed, and I asked Swamiji if Adi's sibling would be a girl or a boy. He said, 'PB if you look at Ma Yashoda, then a beautiful daughter, a Lakshmi swaroopa, will be born. If you look at Sri Krishna's form of a child, then you will be blessed with a boy.'

Every so often I would think Ma Yashoda extremely beautiful, but I was more attracted to the naughtiness in baby Krishna's eyes and ended up conversing more with little Kanha.

I extracted a promise out of Swamiji that he would be physically present at the birth of my second child as well. Now that he had made the promise, I was completely at peace.

However, I was only 33 weeks into the pregnancy when my water unexpectedly broke. I immediately rushed to the hospital on my own; the entire way I kept telling my baby boy that he couldn't possibly come out yet. Swamiji was away for a short sadhana in an area near Timber Trail in India. I prayed to him, and with his grace, it turned out to be a false alarm. We were quite fortunate as Vivek, our neighbour and good friend in Canada, had visited Swamiji during that sadhana and had shared with me a radiant photo that he had clicked of him. I felt as if Swamiji had heard my prayers and had come to rescue me.

For the past few years, every morning, I do darshan of this photo. I then chant a brief mantra and have a small conversation with him, and only then does my day begin. I had observed that he always took a quick shower before having his meal, and I adopted this habit as well.

Swamiji once told me that when kids are young, they should be encouraged to do three things in life—reading books, playing a sport and enjoying some sort of music. These habits would eventually help them to deal with stress and aid brain development as they grow up. And books are the most undemanding and faithful of best friends. He further added, 'Just as a potter designs and moulds clay into earthenware, children can be moulded when they are really young.'

After his sadhana, Swamiji went to Australia for a few weeks. No one knew about his abrupt plan of renunciation. He had always been a traveller, so we thought he was merely visiting Sydney. It was only when I read his memoir later that I would discover that he was, in fact, saying his goodbyes without telling anyone. Matarani arrived in the last week of October and everyone back in Sydney was pushing him to extend his trip.

'PB,' he told me over the phone, 'everyone here is telling me to delay my departure.'

'Sure,' I said, 'why don't you? We have plenty of time. As long as you are here before 23 November, I don't mind.'

'No, PB,' he said, 'I must reach as planned. 5 November. I'll be there.'

As promised, on 5 November, Swamiji arrived and my

heart leapt with joy upon seeing him. He had so much positive energy and his aura was beyond description. He was glowing with a beacon of loving, soft light emanating from him. The next morning, while I was grating paneer for Swamiji's morning breakfast, I felt a sudden, sharp shooting pain and my water broke. An ambulance was called in and Rajan went with me to the hospital, while Matarani and Swamiji waited at home.

Mithoo was born at 11.21 a.m. I didn't give him any milk even though he was crying a lot and the nurse kept bringing him to me to feed him. I told her that I was not doing well. I didn't want anything to be given to my child before his Jatakarma ritual was done by Swamiji first.

He arrived shortly and held the baby in his arms, whispered a mantra in his ear and gave him a speck of honey. Matarani held him, blessed him and enjoyed the beautiful feeling of being a grandmother again. Swamiji lovingly named him Mithoo. He said, 'The one who talks a lot and speaks very sweetly.' I was relieved and happy—both my children had received blessings from Swamiji and he had named them. Formally, we named the newborn Amit Sharma. The greatest benefit of that has been reaped by Mithoo himself. Since his name is the same as Swamiji's old name, no one in our family scolds him; we are unable to. He is also aware of it and uses this armour rather shrewdly.

On that trip in 2009, Swamiji said to me that he had left a small box in one of the chests of drawers, and that I was to guard it and only open it when he told me to do so. I didn't think much of it, and I had been really busy with the baby. Besides, in the last seven years, he had given me so many gifts that I thought maybe this was just another surprise. I thought that he might have written a prediction for my children or left something mystical for me to find.

And then on 17 March, we got an email from him. He had renounced the material life and disappeared. In the email, he asked me to open the box.

The box had a small note with one of his watches. 'The watch is for Adi,' the note read. 'You can't go wrong. One of your sons has my time and the other, my name.' Drawn below it was a smiley face.

Those were the most difficult months of our lives. Not knowing where and how he was, if he was all right. Not knowing if and when we would see him again. Rajan was completely shattered as he loved Swamiji very deeply, more than anything else in the world. Every evening he would come back from work and put his head in Matarani's lap and cry. Matarani showed great courage, but she also stopped sleeping. She would sit up all night. For five months, she did not sleep at all. All our thoughts at all times were about Swamiji. Even when I was tending to the needs of my children, I was constantly thinking about Swamiji and his well-being. Where could he be now? What would he be doing? Was he all right? These and a gazillion other questions would tire me out. All we really wanted was for Swamiji to get whatever he was looking for.

Though it was not hard to understand why Swamiji had been the way he was, I got my answers in Matarani. Her kindness is only matched by Swamiji's and her big-heartedness, simply unparalleled. During those months, she shared everything with me—stories of her childhood, her siblings and how she had raised her three children. She was so wise and patient, and even though she was going through an unbelievably tough time herself, not knowing the whereabouts of Swamiji, she never let her grief get the better of her. Matarani bore the separation and uncertainty with grace and saint-like calm. I learned to recognize her efforts as blessings and understood that one day, when my children left the nest, I would be in her shoes.

I feel so lucky and blessed that I met Rajan and got married to him. I've always received unconditional love and support from the entire family. Swamiji is are our lifeline. He made me realize that the elusive dreams of having a beautiful life can come true for I have had more than enough blessings in this lifetime.

Eighteen months later when he returned in the avatar of a Swami, it was not an easy sight for us. We had seen him live in the utmost luxury. I had even seen him stay in $3000/night suites in the very best of hotels. I learned about fine dining and seven-course meals only after he came into my life. There was not a vegetarian restaurant in Sydney or Toronto that we hadn't been to. For the first time in 10 years, I saw him without a watch on his wrist. Seeing him draped in a robe, deprived of even the basic comforts, was painful. We all hid inside washrooms and under our quilts and cried every day. We had no problem with the path he chose, but we did not want him to live in mud huts without electricity or a proper toilet.

Here was someone who had always employed an entire staff of people—a cook, a cleaner, a housekeeper—even when he was living abroad. And now, there wasn't even a proper stove at the ashram he was living in. This broke our hearts. He wouldn't accept any material help from us or any donation from anyone. 'Let Nature unfold,' he would say. What baffled me was the need for taking such a radical decision. Everyone in our close circle respected and revered him. He was already a swami to us; he certainly lived like one. He had made it clear that he would not marry or walk the traditional path, and we had all come to accept that.

He already made miracles happen in so many people's lives around us, including our own. I never wanted him to be deprived of any joy, comfort or luxury. I wish everyone got the chance to spend some time in his company to see how selfless and kind he is. For such a soul to not have even the most basic of amenities broke my heart. I even questioned God. What is the point of power when the person we love the most has to live so austerely? And believe it or not, Swamiji has always had powers.

I remember this one time—Adi had developed a terrible sty, a boil, on his eyelid. He was around four years of age. First, the GP treated him, but when it didn't get any better, he was referred to an eye specialist. The specialist told us that we had to give hot compresses as many times a day as we could. Adi would cry when a cloth dipped in hot water was repeatedly made to touch his lower eye. Six weeks went by, but the sty did not improve. If anything, it got worse. I was really worried. At the second appointment with the specialist, he prescribed medication and said that hot compresses were the only way, and if things didn't improve, they would remove the boil surgically. It was a sty but not exactly a typical one, he said, rather confusingly.

We were due for the third appointment when Swamiji visited Toronto for about 10 days on a business trip. He gently gave hot compresses to Adi who was much happier to receive them from him. The two of them sort of made a game out of it. He also accompanied me for the visit to the specialist. This time, the doctor said that they would have to operate and remove the sty surgically. He changed the medication and said that only a very tiny scar would be visible, which would fade over time since Adi was so young. My heart was in my mouth, but I kept quiet.

In the evening, Swamiji was giving Adi hot compresses, and I had just returned from collecting his prescription from the pharmacy. Suddenly, seeing my son in such pain, I couldn't control myself and broke into tears.

Rajan tried to pacify me, but I was inconsolable. Adi had been a very patient child. He also had asthma, and now seeing him suffer from one more thing was too much for me to bear. He had had the sty for over five months now. Seeing how I wouldn't stop crying, Swamiji got up.

'What's the matter?' he said.

'Please,' I said, 'you can do anything. Just fix his eye.'

I don't know what kind of a mood he was in but rather than reasoning with me or placating me, he said, 'Have you got his medication?'

I immediately gave him the bag that was sitting on the kitchen table. He grabbed the bowl of hot water he had been using for the compresses and drained it down the sink. Then, he called Adi and blew on his eye.

'*Lai, babeyan ne phook maarti. Ki yaad karengi,*' he said in Punjabi. (See, the sadhu has blown on it. You will remember this one day.)

'He'll be okay now?' I asked excitedly.

'Throw the damn medicine in the bin,' he said. 'Stop all treatments and hot compresses. Do nothing. He'll be totally fine within seven days.'

The very next day, the sty started shrinking, and in less than a week, it disappeared, as if it had never even existed. Two weeks later, I still went ahead with the appointment with the specialist. Swamiji was already back in India and I took Adi to the specialist who was very pleased to see Adi's eye fully cured.

'I told you that hot compresses were the only way,' he said to me. 'And the medication worked. See, you were worrying over nothing.'

'It wasn't the medication or the compresses, Doctor,' I said. 'I stopped doing that on the day of our last appointment.'

'Then why are you here?' he asked, visibly upset.

'I've just come to tell you that your medicines did not work. And earlier, I had said that the hot compresses weren't doing him much good, either, but you kept instructing me to increase the number of applications.'

'Lady,' he said, 'you are wasting my time.'

Later, he even called up my family doctor to tell him what a nut case I was. But tell me, would you agree with that assessment?

What I really mean to say is that Swamiji had always been a saint. It's not just me, hundreds of people who knew him before he put on the ochre robe will tell you the same thing. Ask anybody.

Even when he was away for his sadhana, when I didn't know how to reach out to him, he would appear in my dreams. This one evening, I was very tired and took a power nap. Rajan had gone out and taken the boys with him to give me a well-deserved break. A home with three children might be noisy, but a home with three boys (my husband being the the third one) is practically out of control. I was barely five minutes into my nap when Swamiji came into my dream to tell me that Matarani was having a surgery, and since he was away, he needed me to call and check up on her. 'Tell her that I'm with her and she'll be perfectly fine,' he said. Matarani? Surgery? This was in November 2009. I was startled and immediately called my in-laws' Patiala residence. It was around 8 a.m. in India, and Pitashree had been planning to take Matarani to the hospital. She was to undergo an emergency surgery, a major one. They were just rushing out. The family was shocked to know that I knew about the surgery, not to mention the startling manner in which I had come across this information. Matarani was not in a position to talk, she was in a bad condition. Pitashree didn't speak to anyone, including Rajan, until after the surgery. That's when he called my sister-in-law and informed her that they were in the hospital. Rajan remained awake, waiting for their call and spoke to him around 1 a.m. Toronto time.

When Matarani regained consciousness and could talk, I spoke to her and told her about the dream. 'I tried hard to not think of Swamiji,' she said. 'I didn't want his sadhana to be affected by my negative energy. But he knows. He's always known. And I have always known who he is.'

On a different, lighter note, I distinctly remember one of the dreams I had in May 2010. I had been studying for my Canadian driving test. I had twice failed the test in Sydney, but after a while in a new country, I decided to confront my fears and take it once again. I took lessons every week for 45 minutes.

Swamiji had always had an exquisite collection of expensive fountain and ballpoint pens. To him they were tiny objects of sheer delight with barrels of ink inside them. His collection included pens from Faber Castell, Caran d'Ache, Montblanc and some other difficult names that I can neither remember nor pronounce. He also had a limited-edition Porsche pen that he used the most. What's incredible is that if anyone at any time expressed how much they loved a certain pen, he would give it to them right then and there. Those who have observed Swamiji from close quarters know two distinct things about him. First, when it comes to giving, he is very prompt and detached. Second, none of us can persuade him to watch out for himself and save something for his future or old age. He gives away like there is no tomorrow.

But I digress. So, the night before my test, Swamiji came in my dream and signed a big yellow paper with one of his pens, and the dream ended there. I was so excited that I called Matarani and shared this dream with her the next morning. As soon as she heard it, she said that Swamiji had given me his blessings.

'Don't worry,' she said, 'now you will definitely pass the test.'

I took her blessings and went for my test. Though I was nervous going in, Swamiji's appearance in my dream gave me the confidence I needed. It's no surprise that I aced the test and got my driver's license.

During the months that Swamiji was gone, I continued to see him in my dreams. Sometimes, he talked and other times, he remained silent. Over the years, I've had many dreams of

Swamiji but since he returned from the Himalayas nearly 10 years ago, things have been somewhat settled and quiet. So I was most surprised when in June 2020, I had a strange dream about Swamiji's health. Following which, he said he had a very bad toothache, and he couldn't go to the dentist either. In the dream, I simply went to my kitchen and began to cook lentils and soft cauliflower for him, worried about what he could or could not eat.

I awoke in the early hours of the morning, extremely worried. I quickly emailed him. To my great astonishment, Swamiji wrote back saying he did indeed have a toothache, but due to Covid restrictions, a visit to the dentist wasn't easy. It was a very unusual dream, hard for me to understand and rather unsettling. The next morning, I prayed to Lord Sri Hari to take care of his health, just as Swamiji takes care of all his loving devotees.

Before I end this chapter, I have to share a very recent experience with you.

In November 2020, my father was diagnosed with advanced-stage cancer of the mouth. Doctors had given him days to live. Amidst a raging pandemic, I rushed to India to be at his side. I had with me a rudraksha, consecrated by Swamiji. We went ahead with the surgery but against all the doctors' guidance and advice, we did as Swamiji told us, which was to not do any chemotherapy or radiation. Rarely does he tell anybody to not go ahead with a treatment but when he does, he knows exactly what he's doing. And miracles of miracles, my ailing father, who had arrived home from the hospital in a wheelchair with tubes sticking out from at least four places in his body, now chews food and goes about leading life in a perfectly normal way. He is even able to ride a scooter on his own!

Swamiji's one word brought my father back from the brink of death. My family was deeply affected by this experience. So much so that my own parents pray to Swamiji every day. My deeply religious mother and my not-so-religious father, both born into a Sikh family, listen to the Sri Hari Aarti and Lalita Sahasrnama. How could they not? When Swamiji beckons, even stones melt.

I wish I could tone down my sentiments and appreciation for Swamiji, but I could only do so to a tiny fraction. He has done countless things for the world. I have seen with my own eyes numerous miracles that remind me, at every moment, what an incredible blessing it is to live in the same era as him. Forget his physical presence, even the mere thought of him soothes my soul and brings a smile to my face.

I am reminded of one of Swamiji's favourite passages from *Gitanjali* by Rabindranath Tagore:

Thou hast made me endless, such is thy pleasure.
This frail vessel thou emptiest again and again,
and fillest it ever with fresh life.
This little flute of a reed thou hast carried over hills
and dales,
and hast breathed through it melodies eternally new.
At the immortal touch of thy hands my little heart
loses its limits in joy and gives birth to utterance
ineffable.
Thy infinite gifts come to me only on these very
small hands of mine.
Ages pass, and still thou pourest, and still there is
room to fill.

This could easily be my prayer to Swamiji. In fact, I believe it is. I have come to learn that if there is a person in the universe that you can count on, it is him.

Thank you Swamiji for always protecting me and my family. I earnestly wish that if I were born again, I would become a tree providing you with shade as you sit and meditate, with every breath until I perish.

The Blessing

Zack Bazarnick

May 2017

I spent most of my school-age years in the Santa Cruz mountains of California. My family had settled there to be near Baba Hari Dass, a master yogi from Almora, India. The proximity to Baba and my early spiritual experiences impacted me deeply as a child and served as the catalyst to kindle my spiritual quest later in life. I received my undergraduate degree in economics, earned an MBA and began working as a management consultant. Soon thereafter, I met my life partner, and today we are raising our three young kids together.

The 'corporate life' did not offer me the fulfilment and contentment I had hoped for. I gave it up to be a full-time, stay-at-home dad and would often joke that my kids were the best bosses I've ever had. Two years ago, I found my guru in Om Swami, and since then I have dedicated a significant amount of time to meditation. Swamiji came into my life at a time when my spiritual mentor, Baba Hari Dass, whom I had known and loved since childhood, was very sick.

He had experienced a 'brain event', which we assumed was a stroke as his cognitive skills had begun to decline. He was no longer meeting people for individual meetings like he always had in the past. This triggered a resurgence in my spiritual desire. The thought of losing him brought forth very intense feelings of longing, homesickness and nostalgia for the time I had spent with him. I would go to sleep in tears, thinking I would never find anyone like Baba Hari Dass again.

And so the day I googled 'enlightened spiritual masters', I had no great hopes. I came across the usual names that I was familiar with but felt no connection to. I was a few pages deep into my search, when I came across one of Swamiji's YouTube videos. I watched it with great interest and was quite captivated from the get-go. Over the next few days, I continued watching more videos, and also came across *os.me,* his blog on spirituality and wellness. The very next day, I ordered every book that Swamiji had written, including *Om Swami: As We Know Him*, written by two of his closest disciples.

In the following couple of months, I found myself consuming everything Om Swami had ever published. I watched every single YouTube video, starting from the earliest released recording, all the way to the present. I read every blog post, in chronological order, and read every book. By that time, I had developed very strong emotions for this monk, a person I had never met. It was like I was made of dry grass and twigs, and this newly-discovered material on Om Swami was the match that set me aflame into a raging fire of devotion. I certainly questioned my sanity along the way.

And as luck would have it, Swamiji soon announced that he would be coming to California in September 2018. I booked my spot and started counting down the days.

Come September, when the retreat arrived, I was nervous if Swamiji would be everything I had hoped he would be. Would he measure up to my expectations? How would his disciples treat him? How did he treat them? The retreat itself was fantastic, and Swamiji looked every bit as graceful and majestic in person as he did in his videos. I observed how he treated everyone and watched keenly how his devotees expressed their devotion to him.

During the retreat, all attendees were assigned a day and group number to meet Swamiji in groups of around 15 at a time. Some were allowed personal meetings if they requested in advance and had some grave personal issue. Swamiji accepted the applications based on his own selection process. I was assigned Day 2, Group 4. The group meetings on Day 2 began and I was very excited to meet him and eagerly waited outside the meeting room. When Day 2, Group 2 was in the room, I noticed that there were very few people around, whereas normally there would be 15 or so awaiting their turn. Something felt amiss and I asked an event coordinator if the group in the room was indeed Group 2.

He said, 'Yes, it is. What group are you in?'

I said, 'I'm in Day 2, Group 4.'

'No, that's impossible, there is no Group 4 on Day 2. Group 4 was scheduled only on Day 1,' he responded.

I then showed him my reminder card which indicated my group and he looked very surprised and started furiously texting someone. Anyone who's been to one of Swamiji's camps knows they are extremely organized, with every detail thought of. They always run on time. Mistakes are rarely made. This had everyone agitated—they were whispering, pointing at me, trying to figure out what to do with me. There was no time to place me in another group as those meetings had all wrapped up.

They were reluctant to put me into Swamiji's personal meeting schedule because he was extremely busy and they did not want to add to his workload.

Eventually, they said I would get a personal meeting and that I could join the queue for that. To this day, I'm told by the organizers that I was the only case where this kind of mistake was made. They had no clue how my card had the wrong information, as there was never supposed to be a Group 4 on Day 2. This was my first experience of Divine Grace.

Monika Verma, an old-time devotee of Swamiji, had planned the California meditation retreat. She later mentioned that she had checked every single table for meeting cards to make sure that everything looked right. She had planned the meetings herself and was sure that no Day 2, Group 4 existed. I was the only one who had received that card.

Monika till date wonders how my card got printed. When she had apprised Swamiji of the mix-up, he had smiled and said, 'No worries, please send him in.'

'I can't forget his smile,' Monika later told me. It looked like he knew what was going on all along.

Finally, my turn came, and I entered the hotel room where Swamiji was conducting his meetings. I sat on my knees in front of Swamiji and asked a question about a spiritual experience I had during darshan with Baba Hari Dass. He responded saying that all spiritual experiences could be recreated and to just give it time.

He then said, 'What I can offer you is a blessing that will help you on the path. Please come closer.'

I edged closer.

'Closer,' he said.

Finally, I moved to within arm's reach of Swamiji and he twisted his hands into a mudra (a symbolic hand gesture) while whispering a mantra. He then put his thumb in-between my eyebrows.

I remember thinking, '*Well, this is nice. He is giving me a blessing. I don't feel anything in particular, but it is kind of him to do this for me.*'

And then, I felt an electrical current flowing from his thumb into my forehead, as if his finger had been threaded with a copper wire.

The sensation did not hurt at all but was powerful, nonetheless. He then removed his thumb and instead placed three (or was it two?) fingers on my forehead, and this seemed to intensify things. The electrical feeling disappeared from my forehead, but this time I felt as though my whole body was being charged up. I began to tremble uncontrollably and could feel my body shaking. I must state that I was in complete control of myself and in a completely normal state of mind. It was baffling to see my body experiencing all that from a simple touch (or was it?).

He then removed his fingers and I scooted back in shock. This whole experience lasted around one minute. I managed to get out the words:

'Do I have more time?'

He said in the kindest way, 'No, I'm afraid we're out of time, is that okay?'

'Of course,' I said and immediately got up to leave the room.

As I was leaving, Swamiji said, 'You have a beautiful soul, Zack'.

I cried for much of the drive home. I was so grateful for what I had just experienced and was shocked that something like this was even possible. It was magical.

In October 2018, I developed severe insomnia. It came on very quickly and had several disturbing consequences. I had never experienced this condition before, but somehow I began to have great difficulty falling asleep, sometimes staying up until 2 a.m. to finally doze off, only to wake up at 4 a.m. or so. I took a look at my life and addressed, what I felt could have been, the stressors causing this disruption in my sleep. I felt I was in a good place psychologically, but the insomnia raged on. Sometimes, I would recall staying awake the entire night. It was as if the moment I laid down and closed my eyes, someone shone a flashlight inside my head. Everything seemed bright and awake. It was a very difficult time for me, and it affected every other area of my life.

I examined my sleep habits and sleep hygiene to see if I could make some adjustments. At night, I ensured my room was cold as that supposedly encouraged sleep. I switched off all of the screens at least a few hours before bedtime. In my zeal to find a solution, I studied cognitive behavioural therapy and implemented some tools from that line of thought into my sleep regime. This involved trying to change the way I thought about sleep, making it less of an anxiety-provoking event. It included only allowing myself 20 to 30 minutes to fall asleep, and if I did not fall asleep in that time, I would get up and go read for 20 minutes, then get back in bed. I would repeat this process until I fell asleep, but this would usually go on until approximately 2 a.m., so it did not seem to help at all.

Often, the thing that would wake me up was that I would have to go to the bathroom around 3.30 a.m., and post that, it would become impossible for me to go back to sleep. I tried limiting my water intake to postpone the timing of this regular occurrence. Eventually, I stopped drinking water after 5 p.m., which left me slightly dehydrated. However, I continued to wake up around the same time, anyway.

I also started exercising more than usual in the hopes that my body would be so tired that sleep would come to me more easily. As a result, I ended up injuring myself while swimming because I was so exhausted and had pushed myself too hard. Furthermore, it did not help me sleep more or better, at all. I was really desperate at this point, and so I went to my doctor. He suggested that I get tested for sleep apnoea. The doctor sent me home with a special bracelet that attached a pulse oximeter to the finger to measure one's heart rate and other stats during the night. The tests came back negative, which made me very upset because I had hoped I would finally have an answer to my sleep problem.

I did not have sleep apnoea, there was no undue stress in my life, no major life changes and no underlying health issues, then what was the problem? I was stumped, as was my doctor who then prescribed me Ambien and other medications to help me sleep. While these did help me fall asleep faster, the quality of my sleep really deteriorated. These medications don't really help you sleep and the quality of sleep is markedly lower than when not using any soporific substances.

After taking medications for a month, I was desperate for a solution as my quality of life had greatly diminished as well. It became very difficult to meditate, which really upset me as it was something I had planned on doing every day. I had asked Swamiji at an online forum (Swaminar) if my insomnia would get better—he had said it would. I had a lot of faith in Om Swami, so I trusted that what he said would come to pass.

In January 2019, I made my first trip to India to attend the Chennai Kundalini meditation camp conducted by Swamiji. During my stay in Chennai, I decided to visit a few temples. My first stop was to a Shiva temple. I accepted the help of a guide who had approached me at the temple, even though I would normally never do such a thing; guides often target tourists and it is, in general, not advisable to make use of their services. I, however, liked this man's energy though—he seemed truthful and sincere. I mentioned to him that I wanted to visit a Vishnu temple. He offered to have a rickshaw driver take me to a few more temples, including a famous Vishnu temple.

At the Vishnu temple, I was sad to see a 'Hindus only' sign blocking my entrance to the interior where the idol was kept. My guide spoke with the guards and convinced them to let me in (later, he explained that he had fibbed and said that I was a family friend). When I got close to the Vishnu idol, I started to feel powerful, energetic vibrations. I felt compelled to bow down; the energy was so intense my teeth were chattering. I had never experienced anything like that before. I was not a

Hindu, had no real experience with devotional sentiment or anything that could explain this reaction.

Back at the retreat, I requested a personal meeting with Swamiji, and he granted my request. As I entered the room, he said to me, 'It's nice to see you again, Zack. Even though I see and talk to you every day.' I call upon Swamiji often during the day and I believe he was referring to that very connection.

I was quiet for a moment as I wanted him to talk first. He then said, 'Zack, we all have to go through a certain amount of pain in life. I want you to know that through it all, I always feel your pain and I'll never let you be alone'.

He had addressed my thoughts without me having verbalized them in any way. I was completely taken aback because he seemed to be privy to the thoughts I had been having over the past few days. I was equally amazed at the level of his compassion. I barely knew this monk yet, here he was promising me that he would always be with me in times of pain; that he would experience it himself, as if he were in my shoes.

I then recounted to him my experience at the Vishnu temple and told him how powerful it had been. But I had been questioning whether it might have all happened in my head. Swamiji smiled and said, 'I seat Vishnu at my right side, and if you go anywhere where there is a real bija (seed) of Vishnu's power, you will feel that energy.' He also mentioned that my connection with him was quite strong. It is my belief that it is through Swamiji that I felt so deeply connected to Vishnu. He then stated quite matter-of-factly, 'Your insomnia is getting pretty bad.'

'Yes, Swamiji,' I said.

He told me to take two tablespoons of ghee every night, say 'Om Swami,' blow over the ghee and then eat it. He said this would help my insomnia. As I was leaving the meeting room, Swamiji called me back and asked me to kneel in front of him. Again, he made the hand mudra and placed his thumb on my brow and then, his hand on top of my head. I felt like I was a battery getting charged. On this occasion, I only trembled a little. After he had finished, I mentioned that fact to him.

He said, 'You are learning to take energy in, and this time, I granted you more of it.'

I asked him, 'What is it that you are doing? Is it shaktipat (yogic practice of transferring one's spiritual energy to another person)?'

He replied, 'It does not really have a name, but think of it as blessings and the power of the lineage'.

I felt so comfortable speaking with Swamiji that it made me wonder if I had known him in a previous lifetime. I asked him. He smiled and said, 'Through the mediation you are doing, you will find one half of the answer to this question, and I will tell you the other half.' I was very excited to hear his response, though it is quite a puzzle! I'm still working on discovering my half of the answer.

When I reached home, the immediate thing to do was to try his remedy for insomnia. I had some doubts in my mind, but I also had great faith in Swamiji. I thought the remedy would probably help, but I wasn't prepared for just how potent it would be. The second night after returning from India, I did as he had asked—I melted the ghee in a pan, whispered

'Om Swami' on it, cooked some bread in it and then ate it.

That night, for the first time in months, I fell asleep at a normal time and slept through the night for seven hours! Since then, I have not had any bouts of insomnia. (I have, however, eaten a lot of ghee!) The light that used to turn on inside my head at bedtime was gone, and I would drift off to sleep in no time at all every night since that day.

There have been many times when I have thought, *Maybe it's a placebo effect.* This would make me nervous, and I would think that my lack of faith could perhaps render the remedy useless. I would wonder if the anxiety over this thought would keep me awake all night. That if I questioned it, would probably stop working. Yet even during those periods of doubt, his blessing never failed me. His name, 'Om Swami', never failed me. I am eternally grateful as this was a truly difficult phase of my life. The insomnia had come on quickly, forcefully and with many health consequences for me.

I have in my possession a picture of myself as a child sitting with Baba Hari Dass. The experience of growing up in his presence planted a seed that Swamiji is nourishing into a sapling. In the book *Everyday Peace: Letters for Life*, written by Baba Hari Dass, I came across a letter that Babaji had written to a five-year-old boy who had asked him about magic.

The response from Babaji made me think of Swamiji. Baba Hari Dass wrote:

Jai Sita Ram. There are different kinds of magic. One magic is what magicians show to the public. They have several tricks. They can work so fast that our minds can't see the movement. We can only see what they want to show us.

Another magic is to have some mental power, like to know someone's thoughts, or to move things by will.

The highest magic is to become like God. Everyone feels love, happiness and peace around a person who becomes like God. That person doesn't try to make someone happy or sad. Love surrounds him and spreads out like a light around a lit candle.

In all these kinds of magic we have to practice concentration. If we can concentrate well, we can learn the first kind of magic very easily. We can learn the second kind of magic by developing our will. The third kind of magic is attained by purifying the mind.

It's a beautiful letter and it reminds me of the magic that Swamiji shares with all of us. I know he has siddhis, I've felt and experienced it, but this magical ability to make everyone feel loved and at peace is far more incredible. It's something I never thought I would find again after Baba left his body. Swamiji's blessings continue to guide and nurture me. In 2019, I was initiated by Swamiji and took him on as my guru.

❦

Samadhi

Swami Vidyananda

I'm not very good at conversations, and telling stories is not my forte either. I only know how to serve my guru. To even proclaim that I serve my guru, I think, is an audacious thought. All I know is that my days begin and end with him. He is Agni Swaroopa—his form is like the fire that burns the sins of the past and the present. His one merciful glance can grant you heaven on Earth. My most ordinary and humble origins, still make it hard for me to believe that he chose me to be in his personal service. Even today, it's his compassion that melts my heart in a second. Sometimes just as I'm about to leave for the day, after I have served his meal, he calls out to me and says, 'Thank you, Vidya Swamiji, please rest now. You wake up so early to serve me.' He then lovingly waves at me and says, 'I love you, Swamiji.'

I just stand there transfixed by the tender smile on his face and his eyes that twinkle with laughter and love. What wouldn't I do to receive that divine fatherly smile every single day of my life?

I think it would be a great misdemeanour on my part to capture the enormity of Swamiji's grace in a few anecdotes. But such are the persuasive powers of Sadhvi Vrinda that I find myself narrating some of these remarkable events. Our association has grown over the years into one of deep understanding and fondness for each other's peculiarities. A relationship steadily cemented by a shared reverence and worship for our loving master. I often tease her by calling her author, editor, writer, fighter, chef, singer and poet. And so, with such an array of skills at her disposal, I could hardly keep these tales of his grace to myself.

The year was 2015, and we were gathered in the ashram's old meeting room with its chipped paint and cracked walls. The queue of visitors was far less than what we see nowadays. Very few people knew about us and it was a quiet, peaceful period during which only a handful of us enjoyed the company of our guru. One morning, two middle-aged gentlemen arrived at the ashram. They asked around about Swamiji. It was a weekend and they had just driven down from Solan to meet him. Swamiji was seated in the meeting room and agreed to see them. They introduced themselves as government servants. One was a senior IAS officer and the other, a recently retired high-ranking IAS officer.

On entering the meeting room, they folded their hands and greeted Swamiji who was sitting in his asana on a simple wooden cot. The serving officer sat on the floor and bowed to him. As there was no other chair in the room, the retired gentleman remained standing. He then said to Swamiji, 'I have great respect for saints and holy men, but I don't bow to anyone except for God. So if you don't mind, I won't bow to you. I'll just remain standing.'

Swamiji, with his usual humility, was quick to ask me to fetch a chair from the outside but the gentlemen politely refused. As the conversation went on, we learned that this man had joined his friend on this trip as a last-minute thing—he wanted to see Swamiji merely out of curiosity. The news that a young, educated saint had set up his ashram in the hills had piqued the interests of many intellectuals in the state. The meeting lasted 10 minutes, and the whole time this man remained standing, as if he knew better than to believe a young monk who spoke such eloquent English. He said he had met many learned men in the course of his career. Swamiji remained unfazed and treated them both graciously as one does when they receive an honourable guest.

I was very angry on the inside as I considered it a grave disrespect to my guru. We hadn't invited this man, he had sought Swamiji's darshan. Not only had he disregarded the ancient Hindu custom of seeking a saint's blessing, he had, in his conceit, taken Swamiji for just another sadhu in an ochre robe. To the whole world he may be just that, but I am someone who has had the great fortune of spending these last few years around him, so I know better.

Before they left, Shamata Ma brought out two copies of his memoir and requested Swamiji to sign and give them a copy each. Then, the security and support staff came and took his blessings. The gentlemen were happy and smiling as they stepped out of the meeting room. But that wasn't the case with me. I was seething with anger. As soon as they left, I blurted out, 'Bauji, how dare that man disrespect you? And you spoke so kindly to him. Why did you not correct him?'

A loving smile crossed Swamiji's face as he asked me to calm down.

He then said, 'Swamiji, between sitting and standing, there's a third state too—lying down. He did not sit because that is what awaits him. I wish him well, but he won't be getting up anytime soon. I hope Mother Divine protects him.'

With those mysterious words, Swamiji changed the subject. Lovingly referring to me as 'Motu', he asked me, 'now, are you going to bring my lunch or not? I'm starving.'

I remember scooting out of the room, thinking that one moment my guru is the divine master of the universe and the next, he's laughing and joking like little children do. Humour is his shadow—never leaving his side, always present, no matter the mood or situation.

A few months passed and one day, the same retired gentleman visited the ashram again. He was alone this time. The minute he walked into the room, he fell at Swamiji's feet and did a dandawat pranam (full-length prostration). I was completely taken aback as this was the same person who, during his previous visit, had refused to sit down or bow to Swamiji. What had brought about this change in sentiment? I didn't have to wait long as he eagerly shared the events that had conspired after he left the ashram on that fateful day.

The man began by saying that his last visit had come about because his friend had rung him up in the morning asking if he would like to accompany him to meet a saint. It was an hour-long drive. He had readily agreed because, just the night before, he had dreamt of a sadhu. On reaching the ashram, this man was a tad disappointed to see a fair, young monk, well-educated, with an Aussie accent, who didn't meet the standard stereotype of a holy man.

After meeting Swamiji, he had gone home, flipped through the pages of the memoir at night and parked it at his bedside table, dismissing it and thinking that he would probably read it if he ever got the time.

The next morning, when this man woke up and went to take a bath, he slipped in the washroom. The fall was so bad he couldn't feel his arms and legs. His chest hurt badly, and he couldn't move at all. An excruciating pain rippled through his upper body. He told us that he lived alone. His wife had died a while back and his children, all married, lived abroad. No one was coming to check on him any time soon.

He recounted the ordeal for us:

I don't know how long I lay there on the floor, unable to move. I remembered your book that was lying on my bedside table. Swamiji, your face kept appearing in front of my eyes, and I started calling out to you. I said to myself, if I get out of this alive, I'll surely come see you and apologize for my behaviour.

And then, out of the blue, I heard a buzzing sound. I could hear a phone ringing, but I didn't have an ounce of strength in me to focus on where the sound was coming from. I was still calling out to you and the haze in my head cleared a little; the ringing was coming from my pocket. Somehow, I managed to pull the phone out. It was my daughter! I strung some words together, and she quickly called my son. They informed the neighbours and a couple of my friends came and broke down the door to enter my house and get me out. I had been lying there for over two, maybe three, hours. I was immediately

> rushed to the hospital where the doctors declared that I had suffered a major heart attack.
>
> They had to perform a surgery, following which I was in the hospital for nine days. While I recuperated, I read your entire memoir and thought of you. I promised myself that when I got better, I would go and seek your blessings. You saved me that day.

His eyes welled up as he finished, and I could only gape at my guru's grace. It was no coincidence that the man had dreamt of a sadhu the night before and the next morning, destiny had brought him to Swamiji's door. Later, his cries had reached Swamiji who had indeed saved him. The question then arises: why did he fall in the first place?

My master is a siddha-purusha, a saint; he is under the protection and grace of the Mother Goddess at all times. While Swamiji can let these transgressions slide, Mother Nature isn't as forgiving. I have seen similar things happen on so many occasions that I have lost count.

I said to him after the man left, 'Bauji, is it wrong that I did not sympathize with his situation? Somehow, I felt comforted that Nature punished him for insulting you that day.'

Swamiji chastised me saying that someone's insult or respect meant nothing in the grand scheme of things. He said, 'We did not wear these robes so that the world would respect us. Instead, we did it so we may serve humanity. That is our only dharma. And Swamiji, to tell you the truth, I didn't even recognize that man. I didn't even remember that he had stood upright or hadn't offered me pranams. Had he not reminded me, I would not have even recalled the incident. I don't keep irrelevant things in my head. It is only Mother's grace.'

I knew what he meant, but I don't want to hide the fact that, despite everything, I had been quite hurt by that man's behaviour. But then I think, for someone who had spent 10 minutes in the divine presence of Swamiji and was then forgotten by him, this all perhaps served as a greater punishment than to have his heart cut open and stitched back again.

~

Swamiji's progressive and practical thinking can baffle even those most devoted to him. In the summer of 2019, Swami Vedananda and I were to accompany our guru for the Young CEOs retreat in Geneva. Our journey started much earlier as we spent three weeks in Singapore where Swamiji was either by himself or working in silence. During our international travels, Swamiji observed that it wasn't easy for us to run after him, lugging our trolley bags in international airports. One time, while changing terminals, my dhoti nearly came undone. It was a funny sight—I was running at full speed to catch our plane while carrying a trolley bag and a handbag in one hand and my tightly held dhoti, in the other. In the aircraft too, the staff paid little attention to us, the strange men in the ochre vastras (robes), perhaps taking Swami Vedananda and I to be simpletons from a village.

But it was the comic sight of me running while trying to keep my dhoti from coming undone that was the last straw. When we reached Singapore, the first thing that Swamiji uttered was, 'It's not practical or comfortable for both of you to run around and travel in this attire.'

We nodded in agreement for he was right, and we would

do better henceforth. 'I have to find a way to keep my dhoti in place,' I thought. His next sentence, however, shocked us.

'What do you think about wearing comfortable clothes while travelling, Swamijis?' he said to us.

We had been with Swamiji long enough to know that he was capable of shattering all kinds of stereotypes. We were more than excited at the prospect, and it would actually make moving around much easier. Still, we couldn't resist asking him if the devotees would be all right with this change. 'We only care about you and what you say,' I clarified.

He chuckled and said, 'My children, do you know why I never accept anything in donation for my personal needs?'

'It's precisely for this reason,' he continued. 'So I don't have to sacrifice your freedom. It's not that they will object, it's just that when people donate for a cause, they give to an idea, to an image they have in their head. Whenever that idea is shaken, they feel a bit perturbed. But if we are transparent, giving and serving mankind, we are walking the path of dharma. So depending on your choice, if you really do not want to be in robes while travelling, it must be done openly.'

We told him that we only cared about what he thought of us.

'Don't do it because I've suggested it,' he said. 'Do *you* really want to do it?'

We looked at each other and imagined how nice it would be. So we told him that we were totally game.

The next day, we found ourselves in a grand Hugo Boss showroom trying on well-fitted suits. Swamiji stood outside the trial room like a proud father, inspecting the fit, as Swami Vedananda and I tried on different outfits.

He then made suggestions to the salesperson to show us a different range. His face shone as he picked out the clothes for us. Not once did he look at the price tags. An hour later, armed with three suits each, we walked into a US Polo store where Swamiji bought us khakis, trousers, fitted shirts and collared T-shirts, along with the finest Italian loafers in midnight blue. He was beaming like a child when we walked back to our service apartment in Singapore.

'You guys look so handsome,' he patted my back. 'How does it feel to wear normal clothes after so long?'

'Normal clothes?' I could barely string two words together. These clothes were anything but normal; they were extremely expensive. I was stunned by his generosity and love. He could have bought us anything cheaper, but he said that he wanted the very best for his spiritual sons. I thanked him as best as I could, but inside, I felt guilty as he had spent so much money on us. In my entire life of 36 years, nobody had spent such a huge amount on me. And now, Swamiji had bought us all this in a blink of an eye.

He works so hard to provide for us. Who knows that better than me? I'm the one who makes that cup of strong coffee for him as he works through the night. There are the endless meetings, work on app development and strategy, discourses, writing, projects, recordings for audio series and the other consumer of his time—the life-coaching calls with top CEOs and executives from different fields. Even though he works with experts and specialists in their respective fields, with his input—whether it is coding, business or strategic decisions—everything shines more brightly. His brilliant mind thrives on productivity. He leads an exhausting life, albeit a comfortable and luxurious one, all built by his sweat and blood.

Such is the grace of Mahalaxmi, the goddess of wealth, that I sometimes joke that a sneeze from Swamiji, and riches fall from the trees. He is truly a modern-day monk, one who works for a living and provides for his disciples and the families dependent on him every comfort that they could possibly dream of. All of us have the best of the best but have never taken a penny from the ashram or any kind of donation. 'When devotees give to the ashram,' Swamiji often says, 'they are not doing so to buy gadgets, comforts or food for the residents or my sannyasi disciples. They are donating for a cause and every single paisa must go to that cause only. As for us, we must live within our means.'

Almost every resident in the ashram is paid a stipend and, in addition, Swamiji pays salaries to over 15 individuals every month, which includes some of the sannyasi disciples. All of that is from his personal earnings. I have never seen any guru do that for his disciples. 'One day, when I won't be here, all of you should be financially looked after. And one definitive way of doing that is to ensure we have assets in your name.'

In his practical approach to life, hide the most significant lessons of the Bhagavad Gita. A karma yogi, a dhyan yogi, a bhakta—to me, my guru has transcended all these labels to be one with the Lord. One would think every disciple feels the same about their master, that they are no less than God and can manifest things out of thin air. But it's not just me who says all this in an attempt to glorify my guru. A research project led by an ex-Harvard scientist has indicated how unique his brain is during meditation.

In 2018, a young, bright researcher who had just finished his stint at Harvard Medical School, Dr Ashish Sahani, approached Swamiji to say that his colleagues had been studying the minds of several meditators to scientifically understand the effect of this practice on the human brain. And since Swamiji was believed to be an advanced meditator, would he be open to have his brain scanned for the same? In the last 60 years, less than a handful of masters had agreed to have a study done on their brains; most of those brains were no different from an ordinary one. Swamiji immediately agreed and they coordinated with Swami Vedananda, Swamiji's PA. And so, the team comprising of Dr Sahani and two scientists from IIT Roorkee and IIT Madras, made their way to the ashram.

'I too am curious to see what goes on in my brain when I undergo deep, persistent sensations of samadhi,' Swamiji said. They set-up their equipment and put several nodes on his head. They were all connected to a laptop for mapping the brain activities.

What they discovered, startled them completely. The prefrontal cortex, which showed significant activity in the brains of all the other meditators, was perfectly still in Swamiji's brain. Some of it was visible right then and there, and much of the data was taken back for processing. They also did a study of his heart and it was fun to watch everyone's reactions. But the highlight for me was the moment when Swamiji took the kundalini (a latent female energy believed to exist at the base of the spine) to the sahasrara (chakra located in the crown area of the skull).

The researchers mentioned upfront that they didn't want to use words like 'kundalini', etc. and that the research was strictly scientific. This was a view in line with Swamiji's opinion too.

So when I say that he took the kundalini to the sahasrara, it does not mean that the scientists viewed this in the same manner. But what was undeniable was how we all observed the experiment at the time—with our mouths agape.

During the live experiment, they asked Swamiji about his claim of activating any region of his brain with a mere thought. 'That is true, and I say that because whenever I activate a part of the brain, I feel powerful sensations in the associated region,' he said. They asked him how long it would take him to activate an area at will, to which Swamiji replied, 'a few seconds.'

The scientists used some technical terms and asked him to activate the left region of the brain, and suddenly on the screen, we saw that the left part showed concentrated activity. Next, they asked him to shift to the right, and in less than the time it takes to utter one's name, the right part of the brain showed all the activity. They asked him to shift the activity to the rear part of the brain—the result was the same. Finally, Swamiji was asked if he could move it to the crown, the top of his head.

Swamiji sat still, and some four seconds later, something incredible unfolded on the screen. There were five people in the room other than Swamiji—three researchers, Swami Vedananda and I. During that precise moment, the room erupted in astonished interjections of 'Oooh,' 'Aah,' 'Oh wow,' and even an 'Oh shit!'.

Essentially, when they asked Swamiji to activate his crown, the live scan images of his brain lit up in that region. The visuals on the screen reminded me of the lighting of an anar on Diwali. (In case you are not familiar with the anar it's a pyramid-shaped firecracker that launches a fountain of sparks.

The sparks go up in the air and then they tumble down.) And a mere two seconds later, the image resembled boiling milk spilling out of a pot.

The group asked Swamiji to shift the activity to yet another part of the brain and Swamiji laughed and said, 'The milk has turned to butter. Now give me some time to return to normalcy before I can do that for you. Taking it to the crown has to be the last step. The Kundalini has met its source.'

They assigned Swamiji other tasks such as meditating with open eyes, meditating with closed eyes, focusing on a dot, etc. and went away both intrigued and satisfied.

A few days later, they contacted Swami Vedananda and said that the results were definitely incredible, but they wanted to conduct the same tests again to make sure it wasn't all a 'fluke'.

'Bauji,' I said, 'what do they think of themselves?' I was quite angry at this suggestion.

'Not at all, Motu,' Swamiji said to me lovingly. 'They are right because to establish cause and effect and to make it a true scientific experiment, I must be able to replicate the results each time, every time. So I am just as keen to have it documented again and to see the outcome. It can give hope and milestones to so many sincere meditators out there.'

And so they came back again, this time with more equipment. The tests went on for another three hours. The result? Identical. Yes, not surprisingly, they were absolutely identical. I requested Sadhvi Vrinda to source the research paper they published and the findings they shared with Swamiji. Swami Vedananda had access to the latter. Two key findings worth sharing stated the following:

> Normally shift of regional activity of brain is associated with, or is a product of, some shift in cognitive or motor function. We are intrigued by the fact that you can shift the surface activity on your brain without changing the type of mental or physical activity!

They also mentioned:

> Doing a comparison study of other subjects with respect to your EEG we see that none of them have as distinct frontal lobe alpha and theta activity as yours. And your alpha activity is also extremely stable in the frontal regions especially during eye-closed position. Most subjects have randomly shifting EEG alpha and theta activity through the experiment. Two of the subjects with relatively long practice of meditation have stable alpha activity in one region but not in the frontal region.[*]

Are you surprised? I hope not. Because, being with Swamiji for over a decade now, I have realized that he always understates—and sometimes, doesn't state at all—what he can do. And more importantly, whenever he says he will do something, he always comes through. I have come to learn that every one of us knows a part of him, a tiny aspect of him, but no one can know all of him. Just like you can't always ascertain the whole from the parts and just like the parts don't always make the whole, fragmented information about him can never do

---

[*] 'An EEG based Quantitative Analysis of Absorbed Meditative State', Institute of Electrical and Electronics Engineers, 23 March 2019, 10.1109/NER.2019.8717094, https://ieeexplore.ieee.org/abstract/document/8717094./authors#authors. Accessed on 4 October 2021.

justice to his larger-than-life presence.

You can't possibly look at an apple and appraise the particularities of the tree, nor can you look at its bark and leaves separately and figure out that a fruit like the apple must grow on that tree. The situation is not dissimilar when it comes to my guru. You can construct an image of him from one aspect or another, but to grasp the complete picture is outside the realm of human understanding. You can bring three or 300 researchers, there's only so much that the data can possibly tell them. It would be like one scuba diver trying to explore an entire sea.

❦

Healing

Vanika Bansal

I was catching up with a close friend of mine in 2015 at a café in Bangalore when he first mentioned Swamiji. We would talk about new books and spirituality whenever we met. It would bring us some hope amidst our dull, purposeless lives. He had read Swamiji's memoir *If Truth Be Told* on his flight back from Paris, and was unusually excited. He could not stop raving and talking about Swamiji.

I sipped my coffee, half-heartedly listening and distracted by my own thoughts. I wasn't trying to be rude but I didn't want to hear about another monk or yogi who had attained nirvana. We had already discussed so many mystical, spiritual people that allegedly had magical, spiritual experiences, in the past. Did it really matter anymore? I was far from experiencing any kind of nirvana.

For more than two decades, I had been adrift like a piece of wood on a dark ocean, extending into all directions infinitely. I couldn't see an end to my suffering. All those miraculous transformation stories I had read about were not written in my destiny and God, for sure, didn't care about me. It was *me* versus life in the boxing ring every day.

Back in 1994, I stood in the midst of the most defining moment of my childhood that paved the way for everything else to follow in my life, the direction of my spiritual quest and who I was to become in this lifetime.

I had turned eight years old in January 1994, and my father, a highly respected and dynamic colonel in the Indian Army, had been posted to Jammu and Kashmir. For him, his duty to the country was always of the highest priority. A wonderful man, a dutiful husband and nurturing father, he had been in the Infantry for many years. As a young soldier, he had even fought on the battlefield for the country. In 1994, Indo–Pak tensions were at an all-time high in the Kashmir Valley and there was an almost constant security threat outside the boundaries of the army cantonment in Srinagar. My father had decided that he would go alone but my mother insisted that she wanted us all to stick together.

So our whole family (and dog) excitedly packed up and travelled together from Pune and moved into our beautiful home inside the Srinagar cantonment. This new life seemed promising. It was an enchanting and heavenly place. Surrounded by the most magnificent natural beauty imaginable, it truly deserved its 'jannat' (heaven) epithet. It was a blissful feast for the soul.

I found a kind of peace in my heart that I can only call *God*. I had never seen such colours or beauty in nature. The deep crimson reds on the apple trees that dotted the streets, the shimmering orange, pink, yellow hues of the native Chinar leaves, tall brown and deep green chestnut trees, the hills marked with bright, shiny flowers of every shade imaginable and the crystal clear waters that shone with purity. This was the land of 'Sri' (the divine) for a reason.

'I wouldn't mind just dying here, you know? This is heaven,' my father once remarked lightly to my mother on an evening walk, overwhelmed by all the beauty that surrounded us on all sides. My father wasn't the most religious man. He liked to keep things very simple and kept an open and free mind. He would, at times, just wait outside the temples we visited as tourists as we went in for a routine darshan of the deities.

Things suddenly changed though, and he started regularly taking me along to visit the small, peaceful shrine of an ancient pir baba (muslim saint) near our house. As for me, it was a chance to spend some precious, sacred moments alone with my father, who I absolutely worshipped. He was my hero. I felt protected and loved as he held my hand and with great gentleness and patience, answered the many questions I directed at him about the world.

On 29 March, the day before my mother's fortieth birthday, he was scheduled to visit the military ordnance arms and ammunition depot for a highly classified VIP inspection within the cantonment, about a mile away from our home, along with a dozen other senior officers and a lieutenant general who was flying in specially to attend this meet.

I remember my mother making him breakfast that morning, as he calmly got ready to leave for the meeting, going over his papers and itinerary. My summer holidays had begun but I jumped out of bed early, half asleep, and insisted on feeding him. They both giggled at my antics while I stood there, wondering why they were laughing. He was the foundation on which my life stood firmly and I felt invincible. He swung me up in his arms, kissed me gently on my head and smiled proudly as I held onto him. I felt sunshine warm my heart as I felt the safety and love of my father's embrace.

At the gate, he suddenly turned around, as if a bit unsure, and called out to my mother, 'Hey, listen, don't wait up for me. I might be a bit late.' My mother replied unwittingly, 'Don't worry, I'll wait for you.'

After he left, we started getting the house ready for the party we were going to have for my mother the next day. The energy at home was celebratory and silent at the same time. My sister had left for a picnic up on the hills with her friends.

I sat squatting on the mud near the gardener who was attending to the flower beds dedicatedly, watching him intently as he dug up the soil and planted seeds, one by one, in a hypnotic manner. I was snacking on a handful of my favourite pomegranate seeds and dreaming away with leisure, as only a child can afford, gazing up at the majestic mountains and clouds with great wonder. I looked up towards the house and saw my mother standing at the door, holding a bunch of bright yellow daffodils in her hands for the drawing room vase.

We silently smiled at each other, just moments before an unimaginably loud blast sounded around us. It felt like the ground was about to split open. It seemed to tear the skies apart and rocked the foundation we stood on, for miles around.

All the seeds went flying out of my tiny hand onto the mud as I struggled to regain balance of my body and cover my ears. The intense impact of the shock went straight through me, as if searing into my very being. It vibrated through every cell. Shocked, I looked up at my mother. She was standing absolutely still, her face ashen white.

The sound of the blast had now been replaced by the screeching of terrified birds flying away in all directions and a strange dreadful silence ensued for just a few minutes, before the beginning of the high flurry of activity and noise. The landline phones rang non-stop, our batman (orderly) ran out to check what had happened since (in those days prior to cell phones), my mother had been unable to reach my father. We were relieved when he returned to report that my father was just fine and would get in touch with us later.

Though momentarily relieved, a deeper, subconscious perception of things didn't allow me to settle down or believe him. Without any further thought, I ran to the shrine alone to pray—a primal fear beating uncontrollably in my chest. I ran as hard as I could.

I didn't know what to do once I reached there, so I pleaded to the pir baba, to God, to return my father home safely to us. I begged and cried for his safe return. A soldier standing on guard was watching me. He asked me why I had come alone and I confided in him, hoping desperately that perhaps he could do something. He kindly reassured me. He said, 'Don't worry...he will be back soon. Go back and just wait at home.' Oddly enough, this stranger's words had a comforting effect on me. With renewed hope, I walked back home.

As I neared the gates, my heart sank as I saw the activity around my house and the many people milling about. It told a different story than the one I had wanted to believe. I saw the shell-shocked expressions on the faces of my mother and sister who were being interviewed by military officials. They showed my 13-year-old sister my father's golden dial watch for identification as she slowly shook her head in denial, refusing to acknowledge what had definitely happened.

I had come undone; with no adult skills or information to offer, I was 'just a child.' I couldn't bear to be near the crowds and didn't have the heart to try and find out more. I just felt the dreadful emptiness inside me. So I sat silently, observing everything at a distance, watching everything from my favourite spot on the steps in the heavenly garden, which now felt more like a haunted cemetery.

As far as the eyes could see, there were now hundreds of Indian soldiers guarding the borders, lining up with guns and ammunition on the picturesque, serene hills all around me. Even now, when I see hills from a distance, I see them with their boundaries dotted with soldiers.

We were told that a powerful pencil bomb had been smuggled in and planted inside the ordnance factory that morning, which had been detonated remotely across the border. It was an elaborate operation that had been planned meticulously for months by a Pakistani terrorist outfit. Due to the impact of the bomb, the arms and ammunition depot had been razed to the ground to rubble within minutes. And while a few terrorists cheered across the border on the success of their mission, 14 officers and many others now lay martyred for their country, in a meaningless act of hatred; their families destroyed in an instant.

The next morning, we were packed to fly back to Delhi for his funeral. On our way to the Air Force base, we passed the building of the ordnance factory which was now a charred mess on the ground. My father had been here…at this very spot. Where was he now?

Inside the military aircraft, we sat on bench-like seats on either side of the long aisle. In the centre were the coffins draped with the Indian flag. Each one was placed in front of their respective families—the bereaved wives and children of the young officers who had been martyred the day before.

Unable to suppress my curiosity as my knee scraped the coffin, I asked my mother, who was unusually calm despite her shock, 'What is inside this box, mama?' Seconds later, I wished I hadn't opened my mouth. Her reply chilled me to the bone.

'It's Papa,' she replied. Just those two words, and she patted my arm and could speak no more. The realization pierced through me. I might as well have been shot with bullets.

I looked down at the floor of the aircraft, staring blankly through the spaces in its metal floor. Burning, raging invisible flames of pain consumed me. I felt the blood rush to my head and my soul slowly ripping apart. The early morning sunlight fell from the small windows onto the coffin, where the letters of his name were freshly labelled on. It was official. My father was gone.

The self-protective cloud of numbness and disbelief would, every now and then, part giving way to a degree of anguish that had no description in any spoken language. Surviving the moment became the only plan. My father was no longer there to answer my questions, though in that moment, I didn't have any.

As the aircraft gathered speed on the runway, I held our dog tightly in my arms, silently burying my face and tears in his fur, trapped in this surreal reality with no escape. Our life had taken a sudden, sharp twist and turned into a living nightmare in an instant. You never think tragedy will strike your home until it does. I thought my life was over. I didn't know how to live without him. That day, I not only lost the man who cherished me the most in the world, I lost my childhood, my trust in the world and my faith in God's love for me.

I soon began to wonder what happened to people after death. Why were we here at all? That pain, helplessness and grief was my first initiation into the spiritual path.

We all swept our pain under the carpet as if it were something to be ashamed of and to be denied. We moved on with our lives and pretended our souls had not been crushed. It was a coping mechanism. What we didn't realize is that these wounds don't disappear when you ignore them. They fester. For me, they turned into nightmares with dark entities that would choke, mock and frighten me. As I grew up, I started to avoid sleeping at night.

It slowly culminated into a serious sleeping disorder—chronic insomnia and delayed sleep phase disorder—as I kept myself awake, distracting myself with work, phone calls, food, movies, anything, till the sun would rise, and then I would drift off into a mostly restless sleep. At times, the attacks would occur no matter the time of day or night I slept or where I slept, whether I was on vacation or at home. The resulting loss of energy was debilitating, as if the life had been sucked out of my body. All this started to take a huge toll on my well-being and health, and I felt incredibly lonely. It corroded my spirit and I began to feel more like a zombie than a human being.

One morning in 2009, I woke up to work but I just couldn't get out of bed. This continued for weeks. I could barely stand up during those weeks. I had pushed myself too hard in the past few years, trying to lead a normal life, and it had all fallen through that day. I had a nervous breakdown and had collapsed from burnout. I spiralled into an endless abyss, out of control, into the darkest decade of my life. I felt completely disconnected from myself. There was no concrete meaning to my life and there seemed no good reason to exist.

One night, after another important relationship fell apart, I was devastated and was left with no support and no security blanket. Down on my knees, I called out to the Divine. There wasn't any particular form of God that I had worshiped at the time. I had been knocked down and I cried out with all my heart; there was no drama, no bravado. I said, 'God, if you can hear me, please save me. I don't know how to pray to you, but please come and get me if you care. I can't do this alone anymore'.

Soon after, I met a friend of mine again, Abhishek, who said with the utmost conviction, 'Trust me, just read Om Swami's books, it'll really help'. I ordered one right away.

I was only a few pages into the book, but I was already absorbed by it and noticed a change inside me. I felt an aliveness, a freshness dawn on my spirit, much like witnessing a sunrise on the horizon after being trapped underground in a damp dungeon for a long time. This was a feeling I hadn't experienced in a very long time. Within a few hours, I had read it all the way through. I knew that this extraordinary wisdom and knowledge had emerged from the very source of Divine truth. I had no doubt. I flipped the book around and saw a tiny picture of Swamiji printed on the bottom corner of the cover. I marvelled at how young and vibrant he looked and how kind his eyes seemed.

Swamiji looked different from all other mystics or monks I had ever seen—he seemed to have a gentle, kind, genuine and trustworthy presence. Then one night that week, I had a dream that led me right to him.

I was standing in line outside a coffee shop, with a book in my hands, waiting to get it signed by its author. There was a huge crowd around this person and I strained to get a clear look at him, the person I had been waiting for.

Just for a bit, as the crowd parted, I managed to catch a glimpse. I was surprised to find that it was Swamiji, smiling radiantly and absolutely magnetic! I couldn't take my eyes off him. I tried to get to him, frantically pushing past the crowd, but I couldn't.

The dream broke with a feeling of strange yearning.

Despite the abrupt ending, I woke up feeling unusually refreshed, if a bit confused. I couldn't understand why I had dreamt of Swamiji or why the dream had touched my heart so deeply. About three months later, I happened to see a flyer announcing Swamiji's visit to Bangalore for the launch of his new book, *A Million Thoughts*. I had been intrigued by Swamiji after the dream, and so I landed up at the venue.

As soon as Swamiji entered the hall, I stood up in amazement. Even at a distance, his powerful energy vibrated through the room, pulling in and enchanting everybody in the periphery. Nobody stood a chance. My breath caught in my throat. I had never seen anybody like him and had never felt this mesmerized. It was like being transported to another time and realm. He carried himself with extreme grace, just like what I'd imagine of a radiant Greek god. There were hundreds of people who sat absolutely silent and the energy of the entire hall was charged and electric. It's difficult to explain what happens when Swamiji enters a space. It comes alive in its every atom.

I was impressed by the palpable divine energy—his shining persona, compassion, humour, his command over the scriptures and razor-sharp intellect. At one point, I could only see him, as if a spotlight had been turned on him and everyone else just merged into a thick fog.

After the event, some of us lined up to receive a signed copy of the book from him. As I moved closer to him, the synchronicity of events was not lost on me as I recalled the book signing dream I had had a few months ago. As I reached him, I felt humbled for some reason. I folded my hands shyly and respectfully, but didn't bow down as others did. Swamiji smiled as he handed me the book. I took it, thanked him and quickly turned my eyes away and walked on.

Soon thereafter, I saw the bookings for the first Gayatri Camp and Swamiji's birthday celebrations, which were to be held together at the ashram. I quickly signed up for all the days. When I reached the ashram in November 2017, I was surprised and overwhelmed to see so many people at once; I wasn't used to crowds and it took me a while to get acclimated to the atmosphere there. And I had no idea that we could meet him personally. I had just come to bask in his presence from afar and felt a little shook up when somebody told me that my meeting had been scheduled for the next day. I had no idea what I would say to him.

And so, on the following day, as I walked into Swamiji's pristine, fragrant meeting room with my heart beating wildly, I was immediately struck by his Divine presence. It was looming, towering over everything else. It was a powerful, compassionate, and mystical presence.

He greeted me with a very sweet smile, a gentle nod and a friendly, 'How are you?' It was the most normal exchange of pleasantries. He instantly made me more comfortable as I sat down on the rug near his asana.

From up close, his presence became even more pronounced and magnificent. He looked like the perfect embodiment of royalty and divinity. I did my first awkward pranam (greeting) to Swamiji.

I had no questions planned, but in his presence I somehow found my voice. I even surprised myself by blurting out, somewhat desperately, 'Swamiji, why have I been put through all this painful trauma and emotional abuse in my life?' I trailed off and paused to reframe the question. But I didn't have to because before I could even complete my sentence, Swamiji said with the utmost conviction, 'It's not your fault, Vanika.' He paused, 'It was just meant to be this way…' There couldn't have been simpler words and yet, the impact was immense. I felt free.

I didn't know if I'd ever see Swamiji again and so I shifted uncomfortably and opened up to him about the terrifying night experiences, the nightmares that had ruined my life for so long.

I said, 'Swamiji, I feel dark entities attack me in my sleep that try to pry out my soul. I know it sounds crazy, but I lose all my energy and I don't know what is going on. Am I a being that functions on a lower vibration, therefore attracting forces of a lower nature too?' I laughed wryly with some degree of embarrassment and shame at what I was going through and how ridiculous it all sounded out loud.

As soon as those words left my mouth, Swamiji's expression changed in an instant. He stopped smiling and became quite serious and silent. He looked straight into my eyes and said firmly, 'You are no such thing by any stretch of imagination,' he said emphatically, as if speaking to the deepest part of me.

'It is subconscious and because of all that you've gone through in the past...'

For the first time, in a very long time, I felt peace. I realized that he wasn't going to say anymore on the subject. His eyes shone with mercy. I hadn't asked him for a fix, to heal my trauma or put an end to it. I had fought it for more than 15 years and even the possibility that the ordeal could stop had ceased to enter my mind. The fragrance of that first meeting stayed with me long after I returned from the ashram.

I got busy with life, and after a few weeks, it struck me like a lightning bolt. Since I had met Swamiji, I had experienced no night attacks. I also felt scared to hope that it was finally over. It had happened many times before—the attacks would vanish for a while and then reoccur with greater frequency. After a few months though, I realized they had indeed stopped and had completely disappeared from my life.

There had also been an instance when I had felt like I was about to have a nightmare, but I was lucid and had immediately called out to Swamiji. Most miraculously, I saw him standing right there in my room. And that was that. I'm not sure what those experiences were. PTSD, panic attacks or my own inner demons. I just knew that Swamiji had quietly taken away the long, torturous battle that I had been fighting all alone.

~

I met Swamiji again on 1 April 2018, this time prepared and armed with questions. And I finally decided to come to grips with what had haunted me my whole childhood: the loss of my father. I confided in him on how I had received no closure, never having seen his body or receiving any kind of a message from him. I had been tormented for 25 years; I didn't know whether my father was okay in the afterlife or not.

I said, 'Swamiji, I don't have any closure. I have been searching for answers but I haven't gotten any. Please tell me, is he doing okay?'

Swamiji had been silent all this while, listening to me with great attention. Nobody had ever heard me out like that before. He looked up momentarily, just for a second, and said deeply and meaningfully, 'Vanika, let go. He is fine.'

Swamiji smiled compassionately and gave me time to process this in his powerful presence. I felt like the massive mountain that I had been buried under had been lifted off me. Emotions started to flow from within, as if they too were tired of being trapped inside me.

'Swamiji, I have let go of much of my baggage, but I'm struggling with letting go and forgiving my father's murderers.' I recoiled at the apparent anger in my voice and at the last word I had used so strongly in his Divine presence. I wondered what he'd think of my rage. It wasn't a very spiritual thing to do, I thought.

It felt strange to hate with such vengeance for I had never before that moment allowed myself to feel that way. I quickly apologized to him.

'I'm sorry. I know "murderers" is a very strong word, Swamiji.'

But without missing a beat, he validated my feelings and said calmly, in a matter-of-fact tone, 'But they are murderers.' He gave me permission to feel the anger I had denied myself for so long.

As the old grief resurfaced, it was like I was feeling or talking about things that had happened decades ago. I was, once again, standing in the shoes of the eight-year-old child I had been. I wanted to forgive the terrorists for killing the man who had mattered the most to me in the world, but I felt helpless. I said to Swamiji, 'I don't want to carry this grudge and anger against them for the rest of my life, or worse, across lifetimes. I want to just let it go, but I don't know how to.'

Swamiji replied, after thinking for a second, 'Would you like a more practical solution? I said, 'Yes, please Swamiji, anything.'

He suggested that I could read up on the facts of the political history of Kashmir objectively and see how none of it was personal. It was a fight in the name of religion and politics that had been going on for a very long time. As I listened to him, even in the depths of the pain I was feeling inside, a part of me managed to feel awe and marvel at the extent of his knowledge on the subject. He spoke about it from memory, effortlessly and with great clarity. I wanted to hold onto every word he was saying, but I couldn't.

As soon as Swamiji looked at me, waiting for my response, I burst out desperately.

'Swamiji, I've tried reading about it at times, but it hurts a lot. But your words make an impact on me. So if you were to simply ask me to let it go, I know I would be able to do so.'

At this point, Swamiji became silent and closed his eyes for a few seconds. It hit me that I had asked him for something that wasn't as simple as I had believed. At the time, I didn't know that any word that came out of his mouth had the potential to have eternal repercussions in the karmic play of destiny, time and space. Had I known, I probably wouldn't have said anything. But the plea had naturally travelled from the depths of my being to him.

Swamiji opened his eyes to look at me and there was complete silence. I was absolutely on the edge. Just at that moment, Swamiji's devoted PA, Swami Vedananda, knocked on the door to let us know that the allotted time for the meeting was over.

I looked up at Swamiji, feeling a bit like a deer in the headlights. Thankfully, Swamiji politely asked him to return sometime later. He joked with him, saying there was a very important 'business deal' going on between us. It immediately broke the tension in the meeting room and I felt I could relax.

Then everything went very quiet as the energy in the meeting room transformed. I felt like I was surrounded by a great force. Swamiji looked at me kindly, but his eyes were mighty and powerful. He had a very focused gaze; it was as if a laser beam had gone straight through my soul. I barely breathed. Swamiji seemed to have become a more ancient presence now. It was the safest I had ever felt in a long time.

Without moving his gaze, he said slowly, gently and with great precision in his deep voice, 'Vanika, let it go.'

Then, with more gravity, and even greater emphasis, 'Vanika, let it go.' He then fell silent and so did I.

As I got up to leave, I bowed down to him. I heard Swamiji softly say, 'I'll take care of it.' And he did. He took care of everything. I'll never forget the way he said those words with such finality and care.

As time passed, I have increasingly found more peace and closure. And amazingly, my mother recently found letters from my father locked away in her cupboard inside a bag she rarely opened. She hadn't realized that they were in there; she just happened to chance upon them. That day, she had felt a voice inside her, guiding her towards those papers. Many of the letters were addressed to my sister and I, from when we were kids. I had craved for something like this for so many years. And here they were—a heap of letters lying right under our clueless noses. Twenty-six years later, those letters have brought so much joy and healing to our hearts. They connected us back to our father in a way we had forgotten. I know in my heart, without a doubt, that it was Swamiji's grace and blessings that turned the tides. This was no coincidence. It helped me find my way back to myself.

In May 2018, I was greatly inspired and moved by Swamiji's blog posts, each one a powerhouse of wisdom and brilliance that opened my mind and heart. One fine day, I had a strong desire to compile those posts for my own reference. I wanted to open it up like a scripture or holy book.

Therefore, it was a great blessing that I could gift this compilation to Swamiji on Guru Purnima on 18 July. All I wanted was the smile it brought to his face. Greatly surprised, he said he had no idea that he had already written so much. The book was almost 900 pages long! Swamiji went many steps ahead and brought it along with him to the discourse that evening. He praised the effort and said that it had deeply touched his heart.

It restored my self-esteem, brought me joy, hope and so much happiness and healing. Nothing goes unnoticed by him, and nothing moves him like sincere devotion from the heart.

I started to pray and tried my best to practice Swamiji's teachings in my everyday life. I knew my priorities now. Slowly and steadily, over the course of two years, I started to find myself transforming into a slightly better version of myself, and the scattered pieces of my life started to come together like a jigsaw puzzle.

On 9 February 2020, I reached the ashram to attend the open event, and the Shivaratri and Nav Durga Sadhana celebrations. I planned to stay there for two months. At this point, I had been feeling unsure of where I stood in my life. Was I progressing spiritually? Was I being delusional?

Out of the blue, in mid-March, I received an email from Sadhvi Vrinda Om to meet with her the next day. It was titled, 'Surprise!' That entire night, I tried to guess what the surprise could be but I couldn't have possibly been prepared for the gift she brought me. It was a divine message. The first question that she smilingly and playfully asked me was, 'Vanika what have you been praying for?' Taken by surprise, I didn't have a coherent answer. My heart was beating hard and fast.

She told me that Swamiji would soon have a word with me about an opportunity to work for him. I was stunned out of my mind and barely registered anything, so much so that I requested her to repeat everything she had said the next day. This was huge—all my prayers being answered, right in front of my eyes. I pinched myself to check if I was dreaming, but it was all real. I had expressed my desire to serve Swamiji and to be in Sri Hari's presence at the ashram, silently and only in my prayers. Somehow, my prayers had been answered. Sadhviji knew exactly what I had been praying for, and she told me as much. I was ecstatic at the way things were turning out. I felt nervous, excited and alive, all at once.

A few days later, Swamiji called me and Sadhviji for a meeting and assigned me an important service, one that I could only dream of. 'I wish to build a personal research team that can help me sift through more material. Is this something you would be willing to try?' It was all really happening! In one second, Swamiji had flipped my destiny. He also allowed me to be a part of the ashram family and become a bonafide resident there. The surprise element of this reality had exceeded even my wildest dreams and prayers. Swamiji said that he had noticed that I used to take notes quietly in the corner of the temple during his discourses, and that it had not escaped his attention.

However, during the self-purification event held at the ashram in April 2020, self-doubt consumed me and I realized my past wounds were bubbling up to the surface again. So I did what I knew was my best and only course of action. I prayed to Swamiji to rid my heart of all the heavy insecurities that no longer belonged there. That afternoon, I slipped into a vivid dream.

I was standing outside the Garb Graha (inner sanctum) of the temple. I somehow knew, even in that state of consciousness, that non-sannyasis were meant to stay outside the gate to maintain sanctity of the premises.

The temple looked different, larger and more ancient, with enormous grey stone columns and pillars. Sri Hari stood there shining in his towering black stone form, and I forgot everything else. He stood there smilingly radiant and so alive. I sat on the steps to admire the form of the Lord. Sadhviji too, sat right beside me.

Just then, not two feet away from where we sat, the form of Bal Gopala magically materialized in black stone right in front of Sri Hari's idol. The baby cried and fussed sweetly. And two seconds later, he transformed into a small lion cub (also made of black stone), yawning and stretching its paws.

It was an absolutely delightful vision. But it didn't stop there. I simply watched in awestruck silence. From the small cub emerged a huge lion which roared, alive in its stone form. I trembled as it consumed the smaller cub and finally all forms merged into one Divine form—the Lord Narasimha in all His glory.

He was royal and majestic beyond compare. I could only stare at this grand form. He was so close I could've touched Him. He was immense and He roared with all His might as He looked at me. I felt intimidated. I felt blessed. He was there to protect me.

It was a sight to behold. Sri Hari's idol too had transformed and now stood proudly dressed and chiseled into the form of Lord Narasimha. He roared again, and I trembled. When I woke up, I realized I was still trembling.

Swamiji's grace turned my life—what had once been a living nightmare—into a blessed dream. He not only saved my life, but gifted me an altogether new one. In Swamiji, I found not only my guru, but my father, my mother and God, all embodied in one perfect form.

Sadhvi Vrinda Om once said to me, at a moment when I was experiencing great insecurity, 'Vanika, he is the only constant in the Universe...' I now know that statement to be the most sacred truth. It is indeed an irony that the spiritual quest that had begun with the greatest act of hatred in my life, ultimately led me to the doorstep of the greatest devotion. I humbly offer my whole heart and soul at the holy feet of my guru.

At the Crown

Archana Jain

Dear Archana Om,

Swami will always protect you.

Swami

This was the message penned by my guru on my copy of his memoir, *If Truth Be Told*. He had promised to protect me. And I've never doubted it ever since Swamiji accepted me as his own spiritual child.

In August 2016, I suffered from a terrible case of Chikungunya, which led to a lot negativity in my life. I had prayed to Swamiji to help me get out of that cycle of negativity. And his blessings had healed my suffering mind and body.

Due to the inflammation caused by the disease, I was dealing with an inordinate amount of pain in the body. I had asked Swamiji if I could seek out Ayurvedic treatment, to which he gave his consent. He said it would bring me great relief. However, quite some time passed before my husband, Pravir, and I could make that trip to Kerala for the Panchkarma treatment at the Athreya Ayurvedic Centre. It was a 14-day treatment, and true to Swamiji's words, I finally received respite from the aches and the inflammation. The doctors there advised me to visit again in a year's time to continue with the detoxification treatment.

In September 2019, I went alone for the treatment as my husband's professional commitments occupied him. Being on my own, I got a chance to mingle with patients from other countries like Germany, Australia, Canada and Iran. Once, while chatting to a German lady who was a regular at the centre, the name of Sreekumari Devi, a Pranic healer and reiki practitioner, popped up. She mentioned that this healer practiced at Kottayam, which was a two-hour drive from the centre. She had been quite fulfilled with her experience with Sreekumari Devi and said, 'There were quite a few things the healer said that were on the dot.' I listened to the German woman's recommendation but had no desire to visit a Pranic healer. To me, everything that I knew to be true flowed from my guru, and so I was just happy to be at the Ayurveda centre. A couple of days later, an Iranian lady who had been suffering from severe emotional issues visited the healer as well. She said she had felt so good after meeting the woman that she wanted to have another session. I was intrigued with the details she shared and decided to visit the healer just for the heck of it. The front desk fixed an appointment for the same evening at 7 p.m. and arranged for my travel to the healer.

I went to her house without any expectations. I was curious to see for myself all that my German and Iranian companions had apparently experienced at this person's hands—how she had cleansed their auras and healed their energies. Honestly, while travelling to her place, I kept thinking, *'Why am I even going there?'* When I finally reached her home, she invited me to an enclosure in her courtyard, while she went in to quickly finish her meal. It was getting dark now. I sat there thinking whether I had done the right thing by coming to this place.

A little while later, she came and introduced herself and talked about her ability to feel, see and hear the energies.

'Your energy is very good,' she said to me.

I wasn't impressed at all. I thought people like this woman probably say that to everyone. No client is going to be pleased if you tell them that their energy is 'not good.'

Soon, the healer inspected my aura and the chakras. She then asked about my nose. I told her that, yes, I had been having some cold and sinus-related problems that weren't going away. Then, she pointed at my stomach region saying that I had some grave issues there as well. Once again she was right, as I had undergone multiple surgeries on my abdomen.

'I'll cleanse two chakras for you and that will help with the healing,' she said smiling gently.

Soon Sreekumari Devi began cleansing the diaphragm by focusing her energies on it. However, a few moments later, she suddenly asked me, 'Are you a devotee of a siddha?'

I didn't know what to make of it and asked her what she meant. In response, she said, 'I keep hearing the word "siddha, siddha" repeatedly. Something is telling me that a compelling energy of a siddha is here.'

'Oh, my guru is a siddha purush. I'm his ardent devotee and he is my God,' I blurted out, suddenly all excited at the way the events were panning out.

On hearing this, Sreekumari Devi folded her hands in

respect towards my right, as if offering her pranams to someone. I couldn't see anyone, but I didn't have an iota of doubt that she was right to do so. I too got up and did my pranams and said, 'Thank you for being with me, Swamiji.'

Tears of joy rolled down my cheeks as we both stood there bowing to that silent energy. I could no longer contain myself and expressed my devotion to my guru. Sreekumari Devi was equally overwhelmed with what she had felt or seen and again paid her respects by bowing to the right where she felt the saint's energy. Something like this had never happened to her earlier, she said. She was now ready to cleanse my chakra.

She stood about 3 feet away from me, pointing the finger of her right hand towards my Manipura chakra (located in the navel) and started moving her finger in circles. And to my great surprise, I started feeling an energy in that area. She then progressed towards my heart chakra, and I felt her energy there as well. As Sreekumari Devi moved to my crown chakra to begin the cleansing, she suddenly stopped.

'I'm sorry I can't go on with the cleansing as your guru's energy is seated on your crown chakra. He sits with his hands in his lap.' I could only gape at her because what she said held great relevance to me.

Sreekumari Devi explained that she was a nobody—she couldn't heal me since my own guru was looking after me. She looked at my crown chakra, bowed her head, folded her hands and repeatedly paid her respects to Swamiji.

'Swamiji is showing himself to me...maybe he wished that some healing should be done through me.' She had a serene smile on her face, filled with elation as she stared at my crown chakra. 'You must be a true devotee of your guru for him to show up for you like this,' she said.

I returned to the centre, my heart dancing with joy and bliss!

When I later met Swamiji, I tried to seek some kind of confirmation from him—if it was indeed true that he sat in my crown chakra. In response, he said to me, 'But Archana, isn't that where you always place me when you sit down to meditate?' And, he smiled.

He was right, of course. During meditation, when I prayed to him, I always seated him at that very location. Where else would I seat the most compassionate person I have ever known?

My Master

Swami Vedananda

I used to be a lecturer at a private university in Indore. The vice chancellor of the university quite liked me and was upset when I told him that I wanted to resign for I wished to lead a more spiritual life. He strongly disapproved of my decision and even called my parents. The fact that my parents fully supported my decision shocked him. My mother had always wanted me to lead a spiritual life and as a result, over time, I had been in the company of several saints. Prior to meeting Swamiji, I had spent some time in a couple of ashrams, with the goal of learning about, and eventually adopting, the life of a monk.

I used to imagine sitting in samadhi or spending time in the sannidhya (proximity) of my guru, who would be an accomplished being, and that perhaps together we would roam about the Himalayan forests. I was deeply influenced by popular spiritual classics. And then I ended up getting my hands on *If Truth Be Told* by Om Swami. The moment I finished the book, I was convinced beyond doubt that I had to meet Swamiji—whom I usually address and will refer to as Guru Maharaj in this book—to seek direct guidance from him. However, during this time, all the spots in the ashram were already booked. I couldn't get the ashram administration to approve my visit. This was in March 2017. A month later, I found out that Guru Maharaj was in solitude and that a meeting would only be possible in November. I spent those months in great desperation, reading and re-reading his books.

I always thought that I would meet a guru, that he would put his hand on my head, do shaktipat and I would become a siddha. That, thereafter I would sit in meditation and enter into samadhi and all the siddhis (powers and wisdom of a saint) would come flocking to me. It never occurred to me that I would actually need to walk the arduous path and purify myself to experience even a fraction of what I have just described. In fact, to my great chagrin, I thought I was already purified.

So in November 2017, I finally managed to meet Guru Maharaj. It took me a few months to get the appointment as he had been in solitude since April that year. When I entered the meeting room to meet him, I was blown away at the radiance he exuded and the overwhelming energy he had. I even felt nervous. No figure of authority had ever made me feel anything like that.

Nevertheless, I mustered up the courage and told him that I wanted to experience samadhi and that I had the full support of my parents. I also shared that I wanted to resign my position at the college, live in the ashram and be in his service. He said he could give me sadhana but the rest had to be undertaken with my parents' permission. He also mentioned how difficult the path of sadhana was and that he wasn't going to initiate me until I was absolutely sure. To be honest with you, I don't remember much of anything except the one feeling that dominated my heart at the time: I wanted to be in samadhi and this Swamiji could teach me that. I didn't think I wanted to serve him per se or be his PA.

I thought, I was not only an MBA graduate, a lecturer, an SAP professional, but I was also pure, accomplished and special. I thought all I needed was the touch of a sage. Worse, I thought I *deserved* to receive that touch and be awakened.

So I went back home and declared to my parents that I wanted to be in the ashram and meditate my way to nirvana. That was all I wanted. I can't say that my parents were alarmed but they certainly doubted my judgment. It didn't matter that, by that time, my mother had even read Guru Maharaj's memoir. I couldn't focus much while meditating, and I naively attributed that to being in a homely environment. I believed I had to be in the ashram to meditate with focus. But then, Guru Maharaj's words would ring in my ears that the path chosen by me was difficult and that ashrams were not the only place to meditate in.

However, I became increasingly convinced that I had to be in the ashram. My parents weren't so sure and asked me to first arrange for a meeting with Guru Maharaj. My father had seen many saints in his life and he was not only sceptical of most of them, but was a harsh critic. He told me that my happiness was important to him but he would not allow me to take such a drastic step until he was convinced that Om Swami was the person I had come to believe he was.

The three of us then reached the ashram and met Guru

Maharaj. That meeting lasted barely 10 minutes. When we returned to our room, my parents were stumped.

'He's the real thing,' my father said to me. 'Forget what you've found. I have found *my* guru.' He was teary-eyed. My father, teary-eyed! I didn't even know that he had tear ducts. We stayed back until after the event because we needed to meet Guru Maharaj again and the only time slot available was three days after the event.

'All my life, I wanted a guru,' my father said to Swamiji, 'but life has given me much more. I have found God.' Both my parents were overwhelmed and were wiping their tears. *'Hang on a minute,'* I thought, *'I am very happy for you, but we came here for me, for my future and my sadhana. What the hell is going on?'* It was as if we came looking for a bride for me and my father ended up falling for her. Let not the humour in the previous sentence diminish the confusion and anger I felt in that meeting. They requested for their own initiation and before we knew, our time was up.

We went back to our room and they were very happy. But I lashed out. I told them, in no uncertain terms, that the only opportunity we had to discuss my future had been hijacked by their self-interest. It was like they had been under some hypnotic spell. They didn't say anything about their son, why he wanted to stay in the ashram and do sadhana, or if Guru Maharaj could take him under his wings. Nothing about their dear son, Vibhu Ashok, and if he had a future with him.

My father promised that he would get another meeting with Guru Maharaj and I don't know how but he was true to his word. And so, once again, the three of us were sitting in front of him.

'It's all right,' Guru Maharaj looked at me and said. 'These things happen. Now, we'll talk about you.' My hair stood on end as I realized that I was in the presence of someone who was more than what met the eye. Here was someone who not only looked like a siddha but was actually one. Without losing another moment, I expressed my desire to experience deep samadhi and that I was willing to meditate as hard as required. I told him I wanted to stay back in the ashram and do that. My parents said they fully supported my decision and that they were convinced their son was making the right move.

Guru Maharaj smiled and told me that it wasn't as easy as it sounded and that he would rather have me go back and really think it through. My mother insisted that they had all thought about it and it was best if I stayed back. I had already handed in my resignation letter to the university. Guru Maharaj said that he didn't appreciate my rash move but since it was already done, he had no comments about it. He said if this is what I really wanted to do, he would help me. He agreed to meet us three days later for one final meeting.

Meanwhile, in those three days, my parents were so in love with the ashram's serenity and environment, so much in awe of Guru Maharaj, that they went to the temple every day and prayed that my request be accepted. When we met him at the appointed time, he agreed to let me stay back for three months and try the path of sadhana. I told him that I was certain about samadhi and sadhana, but he just smiled.

In under one month, I realized that meditation was not my cup of tea. Praying was also not my cup of tea. I did not feel any devotion. My mind was all over the place. Interestingly, my purpose of life started becoming clearer to me. It wasn't samadhi or sadhana. It was to be close to Guru Maharaj. The bliss, peace and joy I experienced around him was infinitely more compared to anything I might have experienced in the temple or during meditation.

And then, I decided to reread the only book by him that I hadn't already read twice. All his other books I had read at least twice, some even three times. *The Last Gambit* was the only one I had read once. So I began reading that book on my Kindle. While going through it, I felt like I was in deep meditation. Call it an epiphany or something else but suddenly the purpose of my life became crystal clear to me. I had never been so sure of anything before.

I sought a meeting with him on an urgent basis, and call it my persistence, luck or simply his grace, because he agreed to meet with me.

'Guru Maharaj,' I said, 'I care not about any samadhi or sadhana. I now know what my life's only goal is.'

'And that is?' he asked.

'I want to be your Vasu. That's all I want.'

If you haven't read *The Last Gambit*, then I recommend you do. Vasu is the young boy, the protagonist in the story. Upon deep reflection, I realized that all I wanted to do was serve Guru Maharaj with all my might. If there was one person on the planet I wanted to be in the service of for the rest of my life, not only was it Guru Maharaj, it was *only* Guru Maharaj.

I don't know how or when the seeds of complete surrender and profound devotion towards him got sown in my consciousness. All I know is that I wanted to serve him.

My wish was granted in March 2018. Numerous people would tell me that no one had got into his personal seva so quickly. Guru Maharaj sometimes takes years before he initiates someone and yet, he had been so kind to me. My parents visited again in January 2018 and requested him to initiate me into sannyasa (renunciation) so I could be in his service without any hindrance.

I've had the extraordinary fortune to be with him 24x7 in the last three years, and to observe him from up close. In my limited capacity, with my tiny mind, I have decided to share some of the many incidents I got to witness in his presence.

What follows are not the fascinating or mystical stories you might have come to expect, but the so-called ordinary incidents of life. Besides, if you know him, then you know that nothing is shocking when he is around. Anything and everything seems possible. You feel in control and empowered like you own the land you walk on. So, rather than any strange mysteries beyond my grasp, I have simple truths and observations to share. You can call it the human side of my Guru Maharaj, his day-to-day life and work.

My role as a personal assistant to my divine Guru Maharaj began in March 2018 when he initiated me into his service on the first Navratra. I no longer wished to attain some exalted state through meditation or yoga, for me, that state was in serving my master. Allow me to refer to him as Maharaj Sri sometimes, as this was the title my heart gave him when he initiated me.

So, with Maharaj Sri's grace, I became his interface to the world, a gateway through which people have to pass to meet him. He made me his PA.

Although my learning is ongoing, if I had to recall a period where I was put through intense training, it would be my first two years in his service. The first year was the most challenging. If I thought meditation was hard, clearly, I knew nothing about being in the service of an awakened being, for someone like that is extremely sharp, aware and alert at all times. At. All. Times. It's like riding the chariot of fire. A small lapse in mindfulness and you are singed in no time. Those who are near Guru Maharaj know that he is a perfectionist and expects nothing less from those who are in his direct service. Mere humans like us, however, can never accomplish the highest standards he sets in everything.

But he does not let you run out of motivation. He knows when to scold you and when to uplift you. The most beautiful thing about Maharaj Sri is that he never stops praising or correcting us; even the smallest of gestures don't go unnoticed. One time, we were in the city for an event and were putting up at the JW Marriott in Delhi. When we were leaving the hotel, as per the custom of the place, the staff folded their hands and said namaste. I was with Guru Maharaj, taking him towards our waiting car and paid no attention to the staff's greetings.

After we had settled in, Guru Maharaj said to me, 'Swamiji, this is not good. They said namaste and you didn't even bother to respond. This is disappointing. You must always take care of the sentiments of others. A saint's conduct must never fall below the benchmark we have set for ourselves. Besides, it's not just about conduct, but compassion. Someone is offering you a greeting, at least acknowledge it.'

I will be honest with you, until then, I used to think that the hotel staff were simply doing their job. I had never looked at this from the angle of compassion and humanity. And that's where Guru Maharaj excels more than anyone I have ever met: everyone feels important and respected in his presence. If you speak to others in a harsh tone or dismissively, it makes him uncomfortable. So no matter how stressful a situation may be, we try hard to be caring, loving and compassionate towards all around us.

At another time, Guru Maharaj was just entering the waiting lounge at the Singapore airport when a devoted gentleman recognized him and came rushing at him. Maharaj Sri heard him out and spoke to him lovingly, like he was the most important person on the planet. He introduced both of us to that man. One thing which is unmistakable about Guru Maharaj is that he truly lives in the present. Whenever he gives his attention to something, it is complete and undivided. The man then wanted to accompany Swamiji into the lounge but he wasn't allowed to do so.

The man touched Swamiji's feet to leave. He then extended his hand to me but instead of shaking it, I did namaste and smiled. The man apologized and left. I must admit that the whole thing was a bit awkward and looked a tad rude. An hour later, Guru Maharaj asked me why I hadn't shaken hands with him.

'Next time,' he said, 'when a stranger extends their hand, you may tell them that usually you do namaste, but shake their hand first. At any rate, never be dismissive about any other living being. You can use your discretion but never be rude.'

~

The next incident happened a few months post my initiation. Every day, there would be a scheduled briefing with Guru Maharaj, and somehow it took me a lot of time to get things right. For instance, I would have too many useless points or sometimes, I missed the more important ones. Once, as per Maharaj Sri's suggestion, I started to prepare a pointers sheet. The first time I prepared the sheet and successfully discussed the items on the agenda, Guru Maharaj applauded softly and showered me with praise.

'I'm proud of you, Swamiji,' he beamed.

My master's praise and smiles give me so much energy that I can give my life to see and feel them.

Every moment around him is full of learning and insights. In fact, with his mere presence and conduct, he transforms you. Without saying a word, he forces you to improve, to think outside the box. Vidya Swamiji calls him Billionaire Bauji because everything is possible, affordable and meticulous in his presence. To top it all, his punctuality is mind-boggling. It doesn't matter what time he goes to bed, his day starts exactly at the same time every day. It does not matter whether he has 15 meetings, his writing, recording, discourses, queries and whatnot, all public engagements will start precisely at the scheduled time.

Even during the days of hectic travel, I have never once seen him skip or delay his meals. There is a time for everything. Not only that, he never lets us delay our meals, either. Even if there is work that is pending, he tells us to eat on time and then come back and resume it. If I have to see him urgently around his meal time or if I have been working onsite, he makes sure that I am also fed. When we travel, he tells us to order freely, and breaking bread with him is one of the greatest joys on earth.

And do you know the best part? He knows all about the different cuisines of the world. Sometimes, there are names on the menus that we cannot even pronounce. He tells us to never feel bad about asking him or the waiter. 'No one is expected to know everything. Just like they won't understand makki ki roti and sarson ka saag, it's perfectly okay to not know what a quiche is. Never nod if you don't know. Always ask.' So if we asked him to pronounce the name of a certain dish, he would not only happily oblige us, but also tell us the origin of that dish, the ingredients it contained and their specific cultural or historical evolution. As a result, by the time the dish would arrive, our mouths would water so much, we would practically be slurping.

Irrespective of where you are, at all times, you are expected to be polite, compassionate and careful.

I remember yet another such incident. I had exchanged some strong words with a devotee in the ashram. It was not the way a sannyasi, and moreover Guru Maharaj's disciple, should have talked but I didn't realize that at the time. It had taken me a while to understand that being his PA was not an entitlement but a great responsibility. So in the heat of the moment, I had not exactly been compassionate, but somewhat passionate in my response. I should have kept my emotions in check and I should have known better. Above all, I should not have exerted my authority and lashed out at this person. At the time though, I was angry and believed what I had done was fully justified. Immediately after that conversation, I stormed off and went to my room. After a bit of sulking, I opened my laptop. An email from Guru Maharaj was sitting in my inbox. It was practically two minutes old.

Dear Swamiji

Whenever you act or talk, please think of the following:
1. Is this the manner of a saint?
2. Does this reflect well on you?
3. Is this befitting of my PA?
4. What will be the implications?

Character. Character. Character is everything. Act like a saint should.

When character is shaky, keep the conduct in check.

Help me help you turn into a fine saint. We shall continue this conversation when we meet.

Blessings
Swami

After reading the email, I was so ashamed and yet, at the same time, I had this confusion in my head: how did he hear of this incident so quickly? He wasn't even in the ashram. I got my act together and along with that powerful urge to improve, I apologized to the devotee for hurting her sentiments. She then told me that after our heated conversation, she had wept in front of Sri Hari's idol in the temple. Those were the early days and I was still unravelling the mystery that was my master, but it had slowly begun to sink in that in Guru Maharaj's absence, Sri Hari's black stone idol in the temple somehow communicated with him. And he knew everything that went on in our minds, hearts and the physical space in which we lived.

Many days later, I confessed to Guru Maharaj that there were so many faults in me. 'I have so many vrittis (disturbances), they overpower me...'

He said something very beautiful to me. 'Swamiji, I'm okay with everything except ahankar, (ego). That does not sit well with me. And especially when it concerns a person who is in my service, I can't let them use their position or power to bully others.'

However, you know exactly what I mean when I say that old habits die hard. I couldn't keep my promise and similar episodes with varying degrees of intensity continued to happen. Over the next few months, as more such incidents came to light, I sensed a change in Guru Maharaj. Although he continued to speak to me, he stopped joking around and was serious all the time. He only talked about work-related things. I was concerned because, deep within, I knew I was at fault.

I mustered up the courage to ask Maharaj Sri, 'Guru Maharaj, are you angry with me?' That evening, he said nothing. The next morning, he said something that became a guideline for my behaviour.

'Swamiji, whenever you behave with someone in a rash manner, it's a slap on my face. Now you decide how many times you would like to do that to your guru.' He went on to share that he had seen the PAs of many influential people. They all had an air of arrogance and were often rude to the people around them.

'I don't want this to be the case with you,' he said. 'You

need to make sure that you are always smiling and on your best behaviour with everyone. This is non-negotiable.'

There were times when Guru Maharaj was extremely strict with me, mostly with regards to my behaviour with others. Even if I had barely raised my volume with someone, he'd somehow come to know about it. At times I wondered who would take my complaints to him. How did he know about all my actions? And how did he point them out to me weeks later, all at one go, precisely at the moment when it mattered the most? One evening, out of the blue, Guru Maharaj resolved this dilemma of mine. 'Swamiji, no one tells me anything. It so happens that I know things that I need to know. Maybe the grass, the birds and the wind tell me everything.'

Sensing what I had been thinking, that perhaps someone would report all the incidents to him, he went on to tell me, in detail, what I had been thinking and doing those past few weeks. He listed every major thought, every important incident, all of which no one other than me had knowledge of. Believe it or not, word for word, he recalled the exact lines I had said in my head.

I had goosebumps and my heart was racing, but I was more relieved than surprised because around him, after a while, things tend to not surprise you anymore. It all made sense now: he knew not only the inner workings of my mind, but was also keenly aware of my interactions with others. '*Oh, when will I be truly worthy of you?*' I thought. He immediately responded, 'Vidu Swamiji, it'll happen. You want to be my Vasu and that's why I'm constantly chiselling away at you.'

As you spend time with him, the most incredible thing you discover is that he leads by example. His conduct and personal integrity, coupled with his vast wisdom, continue to transform you bit by bit. I still marvel at how much he can get done in a day.

When I first started working as his PA, my daily schedule was not hectic as it is now. I would always have some time to while away and much of it went in getting mixed up in other people's issues.

One day, I got an email from Guru Maharaj asking me to share my schedule with him. How do I spend the whole day? He then asked me to start a journal and share it with him daily. In the coming days, I realized I had been wasting so much time, time I could have chosen to be more constructive and proactive. And just like that, my outlook changed and my days became so much more productive. I was getting a lot more done in a lot less time.

'Not only do you have to be effective,' he told me, 'you also have to be discreet. On many occasions, you will have the private information of those who write to me and meet me. At times, you may be tempted to share that information with others. I just want to remind you that doing so is not only a breach of their privacy but of their trust and faith, too. If I ever find out this has happened, I will have to let you go the very same day.'

Guru Maharaj made it clear, in no uncertain terms, that while we had a disciple-guru bond, when it came to devotees and their privacy and faith, my role was that of a worker. 'It is why I pay salaries,' he said, 'because that creates accountability.' I have never seen him divulge details of any of his meetings to other people. It was only after spending time with him that I truly understood the true concept of privacy.

Once, there was an important day-long strategy meeting of Swamiji with the board members of Black Lotus. A few hours later, Guru Maharaj asked me to check with Sadhvi Shraddha if a small snack could be arranged for everyone. As is my habit, I went directly to her cottage and knocked at her door. And as attentive as she is, she was happy to quickly arrange for the refreshments.

I went back to the meeting and updated Guru Maharaj about it. He instantly asked me, 'Did you call her before knocking at her door?' I shook my head and Swamiji said, 'I've told you numerous times to call someone first before visiting them. This is an ashram. You can't just show up at a lady's door and knock any time of the day. You need to call first.'

Another incident that remains fresh in my memory is the one from the winter of 2019. There were some morning meetings scheduled to be held at Maharaj Sri's cottage. I was waiting outside the venue to escort the gentlemen back once their meeting was over. Meanwhile in the kitchen, Swami Vidyananda and Sadhvi Vrinda were preparing Guru Maharaj's lunch. They were merrily chatting with each other as they chopped vegetables and went about their work. I somehow felt that I should tell them to lower their volume as the noise could have disturbed the ongoing meeting. I politely asked them to speak softly.

Sadhviji asked me, 'Has Guru Maharaj asked you to say this to us, Swamiji?' When I said no, she simply went back to work and resumed her conversation.

I was upset by this and returned to my post outside the door. It was with this strained mindset that I met Guru Maharaj after the meeting concluded. He said, 'Swamiji, whatever happened earlier, avoid that. I see that you are angry and hurt.'

He clarified, saying, 'Please always remember how much both Swami Vidyananda and Sadhvi Vrinda love you and care for you. You ought to be mindful of the feelings of the people around you. If you are going to unnecessarily step on other people's toes, you will alienate them.'

~

A couple of months after my sannyasa, Swami Vidyananda and I travelled with Guru Maharaj for an event in Singapore. After conducting a three-day meditation event in Delhi, we reached the airport. At the immigration checkpoint, Guru Maharaj conducted all the proceedings while explaining to me how things were done. What touched me the most was that instead of making me feel like he was doing my job, he simple said, 'Swamiji, this is your first time, so don't worry. Just observe me, and next time you can do it all by yourself.'

Soon we were headed towards the departure gate and a funny thing happened. I was drained of energy and was tagging behind my master like a shaggy little puppy. Guru Maharaj turned around and nudged me, 'Swamiji, why are you walking in that manner? Pick up your pace, walk straight, hold your head high as you walk. Let me show you how it's done,'

And there, in the middle of the airport, Guru Maharaj demonstrated to me how alert a monk must be at all times.

As soon as this lesson was over, he surprised me with yet another thing. He took us to an Apple store and asked the salesperson there to show us the latest Apple watch. He paid for it, turned around and said to me, 'Here, Swamiji, this is for you. I've noticed you like to wear a watch.' I was so surprised and full of joy, I wanted to prostrate at his feet right there. Being with my guru is a rollercoaster ride—he's full of beautiful surprises and it never ceases to amaze me how he keeps everyone so happy around him.

After landing at the Singapore airport, Guru Maharaj asked me if I had filled out the immigration form for the both of us. I hadn't. He said, 'Oh! Swamiji, now this will delay us.' He then quickly arranged for the form and started filling it out himself. I was so embarrassed, for my guru was once again doing my job. We then rushed toward the exit point, but we were already late and there was a long queue in place. We had to wait quite a while for our turn. Outside, a group of Singapore devotees had come to receive us with fanfare. On the way to the hotel, a devotee requested Guru Maharaj to sing a bhajan. He was bone-tired after three hectic days in Delhi and the journey to Singapore, but still, at the request of the devotee, he sang the bhajan.

In the summer of 2019, we accompanied him to Geneva. Guru Maharaj was there to address the members of the Young Presidents Organization (YPO) at a two-day private meditation retreat.

I went ahead to check the audio-video settings at the venue and found that there were a few adjustments that needed to be made. The company's IT guy was very kind to lend me his things and helped me in making the required arrangements.

Most of the people there had never attended a session led by a monk before and had not the faintest idea of what it would be like. When the first talk got over, they were all eager to have a word with Guru Maharaj in private. One of the most beautiful aspects of working under Guru Maharaj and learning from him is that he's a very straightforward person who tells you exactly where and how you need to improve.

It was very interesting to see how my guru conducted himself while conversing with people of different faiths. He was like water, reflecting the values that not only appealed to them but also made them reflect on their set of beliefs and values. Post the retreat, I received quite a few emails from the attendees saying that the retreat had been a life-changing event for them. It had made them rethink their priorities.

The core group of CEOs requested that they take Guru Maharaj out for dinner. A CEO personally came to pick him up. She spoke to him about technology and Guru Maharaj conversed with her just as comfortably. It was as if he knew everything there is to know in the world.

They were so in awe of him that they requested him to speak at another very exclusive event. I was concerned about his asana (his posture—whether he would be comfortable or not) and other arrangements, and expressed as much.

He said, 'Swamiji, please don't worry about it. We are their guests. I'm okay with whatever seating arrangement they offer.'

The UK event was to be held two days after we reached London and fortunately, we had a day and half to ourselves. The next morning, we went to Four Seasons for breakfast. Shall I tell you something interesting? We usually have a comfortable stay whenever we travel for an event and the devotees make arrangements for us. In fact, usually, we have detailed checklists for everything: from the kind of stay we require, the food, to the audio-visual equipment. The minutest detail—for instance, keeping a bottle of warm water at a certain temperature—is covered. But on these trips, Maharaj Sri is most frugal and compromises all the time because each devotee's way of expressing their devotion is different.

But you only have to spend a few days with him to know the level of his exposure to things and the way he pays attention to the details. So the interesting thing I wanted to tell you is that when we travel on official business, the quality of arrangements is very good, but when we travel on personal business, Guru Maharaj makes out-of-the-world arrangements. Everything is the best there is. 'When we are not asking devotees to use their resources, I feel very free. Besides,' he says, 'you are my spiritual sons and must have the best of everything.'

Now, getting back to the Four Seasons story. A waiter attended to us, and Guru Maharaj gave the order explaining to him how he would like his breakfast to be served, placing emphasis on no eggs, etc. He gave very detailed, specific instructions. However, when the food came, he wasn't happy with it, so he let the person know, gently, yet firmly. I couldn't help but notice the preciseness of his speech. But they still couldn't get it right. Maharaj Sri remained firm and asked for the chef. He showed the chef what was lacking in the meal. The chef, in return, apologized profusely and offered a free meal. When the bill came, his item was not charged. Guru Maharaj sent the bill back and requested that his meal also be charged.

'It's very simple, Swamiji,' he said to me. 'I'm dining here as a customer. And therefore, I expect a certain quality of service. Anything to the contrary is just not acceptable.'

After some time, it so happened that I dropped a fork and was going to pick it up, but Guru Maharaj lovingly chided me, saying that alertness at all times was the hallmark of a good monk. 'It's the small things that matter,' he said. Over the years, he has taught me a great many things, which gradually made me more confident and more assured of my standing in the world, by his side.

Even though we were only there for breakfast, Maharaj Sri left a £20 tip for the waiter and he asked me to pay another £10 each to the two security guards standing outside. 'This was my opportunity to do some good in the morning, Swamiji,' he told us. 'What we ate was for our bodies, but what we gave was for our souls. It's the simple secret of the Universe: be competent and be charitable. Nature will then reward you in abundance.' Whenever we travel, he gives me his card, tells me to withdraw money from the ATM and then asks me to give half of that to Vidya Swamiji. 'Consider it your pocket money,' he says. 'Spend wherever you need to.' Even now, I have nearly $2,000 sitting with me in cash and Vidya Swamiji has a bit more.

In the beginning, I used to maintain a detailed account of what and where we were spending, like on meals, travel, accommodation, etc., but he told me that he trusted us fully. In the three years I have been with him, he has not once asked where the money had gone. Vidya Swamiji says the same about him and his time with Maharaj Sri spans over a decade. 'My philosophy is very simple,' he said. 'I'm not a hoarder. If the taxes have been paid, the charity has been done, and there's still money in the account, you can use it for anything good. If nothing is left, either we lower our expectations or we work harder. I have never been a good money manager. I have just been a hard worker.'

Usually we see saints and sannyasis, especially gurus, acting all self-important. But my Maharaj Sri is grounded, without any desire for any special treatment. In fact, he actively discourages it. He doesn't like it when people come to receive him at the airport or to see him off. He maintains that it is a waste of resources and an unnecessary inconvenience to those people. Most of the time, we don't share his travel plans just so that he may travel the way he likes. 'I'm happy to travel quietly and not be known. The thing with fame is that it's quite counter-productive—it doesn't serve a purpose. I am happy to live like any other normal citizen,' he would explain. This humility comes naturally to him.

Many diplomats, bureaucrats and political figures visit him. Guru Maharaj has never asked me to ever take anyone's contact details. He has never asked anyone to take a picture with him. Once, a devoted bureaucrat told me that if we ever had to go through an Indian international airport, I just had to inform him and all VIP arrangements would be made. Those were my early days and I duly informed him. At the airport, we were escorted like VVIPs. Guru Maharaj reprimanded me as soon as the others left. At another time, he had to visit a city for a conference and a senior minister requested the presence of Maharaj Sri as a guest of the state and went far as to extend the government's hospitality towards him. He turned it down immediately and asked me to make sure that nothing of that sort happened ever again. 'I am not speaking at a government event, I am not a politician, I am not a government employee, I have not come for a social cause,' he said, 'so how can we justify using national resources for my comfort? I am happy to quietly get down at the airport and go to our hotel.'

I am not sure what to call this. Humility, principles, truthfulness or perhaps all of these. All I know is that I have never met anyone who thinks so minutely or upholds their principles with such steadfastness.

At times, I feel that Maharaj Sri is just too kind for this world. We find him sacrificing his comfort and sleep so that he may respond to queries and get the work done. When we travel, there are times when the pressure is too much and the meetings unavoidable. While Vidya Swamiji and I are resting and enjoying, he is either attending a meeting or working on his laptop. Sometimes, we feel bad and frankly, quite helpless. On all the trips that I have been with him, not even once, has he gone sightseeing or had a lazy day. I have wanted to say no to so many people who request for a meeting but if anyone is suffering, he tells me it is our duty to make time for them. Sometimes, I wonder if this unreasonable kindness is actually a good thing.

Speaking about this subject, a year ago, in an ashram-residents meeting, Guru Maharaj read out two chapters from his upcoming book on kindness. His writing was mesmerizing. After we reached his cottage, I said to him, 'Maharaj Sri, it's very difficult for me to be kind. Somehow, it doesn't come to me naturally.'

You see the irony of the situation—a guru who stands for compassion and kindness, has his close aide confessing to him about his lack of kindness. Especially, when the guru has only shown love and kindness to him, under all circumstances.

A tender smile spread across his beautiful face and he

said, 'No worries, Swamiji. If you can't be kind, then at least always be polite. It'll come to you. If my tapas is real then one day, you will melt like butter.'

As I mentioned earlier, wherever we stay, in whichever hotel of the world, he never holds his hand back in profusely tipping the staff. Whether it's rupees or dollars or pounds, tips flow from him to no end. When we are about to check out, it is a custom for him to tip everyone in the security and the on-duty staff in the hotel. It won't hurt to remind you that we don't take any donations. Even if someone wants to donate to the ashram, Guru Maharaj politely tells them to just do it at the office when they visit the ashram. All the charity he does is strictly from his personal income, which is usually from books and some from events. In fact, I was surprised to know that he doesn't have any access to the ashram's bank account. 'The trustees are doing a good job, Swamiji,' he told me. 'I trust them. Whatever is in the ashram belongs to the devotees. My heart is in charity and that's what gives me the greatest joy and solace.'

Once in Delhi, as usual, I was assigned the seva of tipping everyone before leaving. But, this one time, things were quite hectic and we were rushing. On our way out, I forgot to tip a couple of guards at the gate. This happened again at the airport. To be honest with you, I hadn't given it much importance in my head. Those were my early days with him. I thought we had already tipped so many of the staff and I wanted to save his money.

After we passed through the security check at the airport, Guru Maharaj asked, 'Swamiji, why did you leave those people out? Why would you not tip them? I've given you enough cash.'

He paused for a moment and continued, 'Just see it from their eyes. They have to struggle every day to maintain a decent living, and we have everything. It's a chance to do some good karma and you mustn't be stingy about it. Please be careful next time. Look at the level of exploitation in our own country. We must do our bit to restore equality in our society.'

In another incident at the JW Marriott in New Delhi, due to some reason, we had to go through a side door where the guard was frisking everyone. When it was our turn, the guard reached towards Guru Maharaj to frisk him. I stepped forward to tell him that it was not necessary. I told him that we were frequent guests at the hotel, staying in so and so room, and that he could frisk me and everybody else, but not Guru Maharaj. He is never frisked when we go through the front door.

The guard insisted upon it and I told him that I was going to speak to the general manager (GM) of the hotel. The GM had personally given me his number to let him know if we ever faced any inconvenience. 'Swamiji,' Guru Maharaj held my arm to quieten me. He then said to the security guard, 'Please, carry on with your checks.' He stepped forward and the guard ran the security wand over him and frisked him a bit.

The moment we passed the gate, Maharaj Sri chastised me. 'Swamiji, this person is only doing his duty; his intention is not to harass anyone. I know your intentions were good. But you must never throw around your weight, particularly when the other person is just doing his job. Please go and tip him, tell him not to worry about anything.' Guru Maharaj told me to tip him ₹1,000.

Truth be told, he gives so much to everyone, that sometimes I wonder he'd have anything left for himself. I've never seen him desiring anything special. To him, money is simply a means to do more charity, make people's lives comfortable and give them access to opportunities they'd otherwise never have had. I don't know what good karma I did to become associated with him. Maybe it's just his grace. He has taught me how to truly love and care for the lives of others.

~

In the middle of 2019, Guru Maharaj had planned to spend some time in solitude in Australia. It was a lovely period for Vidya Swamiji and me as we spent time with our guru, without the stress of any event or private meetings to worry about.

On our layover at Singapore, Guru Maharaj called us to have coffee with him. He casually asked us, 'Swamijis, would you be comfortable wearing something other than the saffron robes when we travel abroad? Like shirt and trousers, a fitted suit, maybe?

I was stumped and just sat there grinning like a child because not a day ago, I'd had that exact same thought. It becomes difficult to deal with matters while trying to run around in a dhoti-kurta. This I could hardly dismiss as a coincidence as Guru Maharaj had surely read my mind.

He asked us again, if this was something we would like to do. To be honest, I leapt at the opportunity, as it would help me serve my master far more efficiently while we travelled in foreign lands. Later, Guru Maharaj also said that people would take us more seriously because the moment they see a monk in saffron robes, they think he's either uneducated or poor, or both. Then came the next surprise. I had thought Maharaj Sri was allowing us to wear casual clothes in ochre or a shade closer to that colour, but he said we could wear any colour we liked, anything that would look professional and formal.

This decision was unheard of in the traditional order of sannyasa. A decision that coming generations would remember long after we would be gone—that clothes don't make a sannyasi, character does. Maharaj Sri has never bound us by any protocols that could hamper our progress.

He is all tradition, yet modern, God-loving and just as scientific. He's an enigma, the perfect balance between science and faith.

He then took us to the showrooms of the best brands out there: Polo Sport, Ralph Lauren, Hugo Boss, Calvin Klein and quite a few others. Guru Maharaj took us around quite like a mother takes her children shopping.

I was flabbergasted to see that one suit cost a small fortune. And he got both of us multiple suits! This went on for a few more days, until we said to him, 'That's enough, Guru Maharaj, our wardrobes are overflowing.' To which he lovingly replied, 'There must be something else I can buy for you.'

I have to admit, it was so easy to move about in a perfectly tailored suit. I felt more confident and efficient as I dealt with people from different races and cultures. While in Singapore, we asked him if we could go to Universal Studios and he happily gave his consent. In fact, every day while he worked away on his laptop, Vidya Swamiji and I would step out to sometimes catch a movie or to just look around. It is of utmost importance for Guru Maharaj that we are comfortable and happy in his service. Being in his service is one of the rarest opportunities—rarest of the rare—that anyone could possibly get.

We soon headed to Australia, where I was exposed to a different culture and environment. For a couple of months, we had the good fortune of being in close vicinity to Maharaj Sri. Sometimes, when he needed to speak to me about something, he would simply walk down the stairs from his study, instead of summoning me to him. He said he preferred to come down to speak with me rather than disrupt my audio editing or other work. It greatly touched our hearts, that though we were in his service as his disciples, he always treated us as his children.

Whenever he walked into our room, we would stand up in reverence, but he would instruct us to remain seated. That there was no need to disturb our work setting. Regardless, the next time he would visit, we would stand up again and so he finally said to us, 'If you are going to stand up every time I visit your room, then I won't come here. I need you to be at ease.'

His concern and sensitivity regarding our comfort and privacy made a great impression on me. Now, when I work with someone, I try and extend the same courtesy to them. 'What would my Guru Maharaj do?'—this is a question that constantly runs through my mind. Whenever he exchanges emails or any other communication with me, every instruction of his, whether it is a question or a request, he never forgets to use 'please'. The word 'please' is very important to him.

On this trip, Guru Maharaj gave me the responsibility of handling all the payments and bills. When I would speak to people, Guru Maharaj observed from a distance, and afterwards he would gently point out the improvements I could make in my speech and approach. One time, after I made a payment at a restaurant, Guru Maharaj said, 'Swamiji, next time please place the money in the person's hand. If you put the money on the table, it can feel impolite.'

Being with him has made me understand the value of small actions and gestures in life. I also realized how far ahead he has to think of us mere mortals. We may not fathom the consequences of our actions and thoughts, but with his guidance and grace, he stops his children from making grave mistakes in the present and in the future.

During Guru Maharaj's solitude in Australia, we were staying next to a beautiful elderly couple named Catherine and Brian. The day after our arrival, I was standing outside our cottage, finishing some work, when the couple came out to greet us. They were curious about Swamiji. I talked to them about Guru Maharaj and they invited us to visit them.

The next day, the lovely Catherine brought a vegan cake and expressed her desire to meet Guru Maharaj. Two days later, Maharaj Sri asked me to invite our neighbours over. Since I was unaware of the customs of the new place, he told me what to say and how to say it. When I passed on the invitation to them, they were very happy.

During this particular visit to Australia, we had to make several trips to the local bazaar and other places to procure groceries, etc. I observed Guru Maharaj closely as he conversed with people from the department stores and other shop owners.

I thought the way he would place an order and respond to people was just so wonderful. I could see how carefully he selected his words before he said anything. His facial expression, body language, everything about him, reflected a sense of calm. Many times, he would let me handle the conversations and then afterwards give me pointers to improve. This gave me confidence to handle people and situations in a different cultural setting.

One day, just before lunch, he showed me a document and asked my opinion on it. I said it was very good and so on. I thought since Guru Maharaj was sharing it, I should say good things about it. Moments later, he showed me another version of the same document. Once again, I approved of the document.

'Swamiji, if you can't offer an honest opinion, then there's no point in asking you, is there?' he asked. 'All my life, I have garnered enough appreciation that I can take criticism in great spirit. It is very important to me that you are able to express yourself openly. I'm not sharing a document to hear my glories but to actually know what you think of it.'

I mumbled a 'Yes, Guru Maharaj', to which he replied, 'I don't expect you to say yes to everything. I would like you to be frank and candid. I don't work with "Yes boss" people.'

This incident gave me a different perspective on life—I needed to let the people around me, the ones who worked with me, express themselves and I needed to take their comments and criticism in good spirit.

A funny thing happened after spending a few weeks in Australia. My accent started to change. I was trying to speak in the Australian manner, but it was evident that I was just copying them and came across as rather silly. Maharaj Sri asked me to speak naturally and said that there was no need to ape the accent. It's a marvel how he points out things so gently that one never actually feels bad. I've never seen anyone as patient as him.

One time, an electrician had come to do some work at our Australian lodgings. It was 11.30 a.m., Guru Maharaj's lunch time, and so he asked the technician to join us for the meal. He accepted the invitation. Till date it remains one of the most beautiful meals I have ever had. Once the man's job was done, Maharaj Shri offered him some brand new items that happened to be lying around the house. Our Australian friend gladly took them and was very grateful for the unexpected gifts.

I've always seen Maharaj Sri take care of everyone around him, even those who appear out of nowhere. He is always keenly aware of what their needs might be.

He often says that the first thing he sees in another person is their soul, the beautiful child within. It's the truth and I've repeatedly witnessed this in action.

Swami Vidyananda and I love good food, and Guru Maharaj made sure we visited all the places that offered the most unique delicacies. Even after an extremely busy day, he made it a point that we enjoyed every moment of our stay. He would say to us both, 'Your happiness is most dear and important to me.'

When the period of solitude was over, we headed back to India via Mumbai. On our return flight, Maharaj Sri asked Swami Vidyananda to meet him at his seat. When Swami Vidyananda returned, he handed me a packet. I opened it, and voila, it contained something I had desired for a long time—a sleek and expensive wallet. This is how Maharaj Sri's generosity continues to surprise me, just as much as his stupendous powers of premonition.

At the ashram, Sadhvi Vrinda's aunt and her cousin were visiting from Sydney and a meeting had been scheduled with Swamiji a day later. In the morning, Guru Maharaj asked me whether I had shared the duration of the meeting with them. When I said no, he merely shook his head and gave me the exact time at which I was supposed to show up.

I was late by a couple of minutes. As Sadhviji's aunt came out of the meeting place, her foot hit the glass flower vase kept on the stairs and it fell down with a big thud. It was only due to Maharaj Sri's grace that somehow she was saved from falling down the stairs herself. After they left, Swamiji said to me, 'You must wonder at times, Vidu Swamiji, why I am so particular about the exact minutes of the meeting. Well, as you saw in the morning, she had to be here at that very moment in order for me to save her. It's one of the reasons I insist you carry out my instructions at a precise time and day. Had you been here on time, that moment would have passed and she would not have slipped. I'm not saying that it's your fault, but please measure the punctuality I require in seconds, not minutes.'

There are times when, out of the blue, Maharaj Sri has asked me to send an email to a person and send blessings to them on his behalf. And later, I've found out that the person was in a dire condition and much in need of my guru's divine intervention. This has happened so many times, it has become a normal occurrence for me. Since the time I have been in his service, I have seen hundreds of people entering the meeting room crying and then coming outside awash with tears of happiness. Maharaj Sri graces everyone with one thing or the other—some he blesses with a child, some are cured in an unimaginable way and some are a lot less lost than when they had first arrived at our sacred ashram bhoomi (grounds).

Once I asked him, 'I've seen so many people forget us after their work is done, then why do you put in so much effort?'

'Arey,' said Swamiji, with a certain amount of surprise. 'What has their gratitude or lack of it got to do anything with my conduct? My job is to indiscriminately help people.'

~

My father was so ill at one time that we thought his time had come. He had been suffering from Irritable Bowel Syndrome (IBS) all his life, but things became extremely dire in 2019. No medication or diet worked. He lost weight drastically and rapidly, and at one point weighed only 34 kilograms. His pulse dropped to dangerous levels and he could not eat. He had been on just water for more than seven days. Just water! I was extremely worried. My family requested me to check with Guru Maharaj as I was in Sydney with him at the time. At first, I told them that he knew everything so there was really no need, but when my father's condition continued to deteriorate, I acceded to their request and shared their note with him.

He read the note and said to me, 'What does your heart wish?'

'Whatever you decide, Maharaj Sri,' I said, 'it will be for the best.'

'But I need to hear it from you.'

'Please save him, if possible,' I pleaded. 'My mother really needs him.'

'Done,' Guru Maharaj said, 'he'll start improving this very instant.'

He told me to convey to my family that they just had to say 'Om Swami', blow on his food and then feed him. He would be fine, he said. He also wrote down an entirely new diet plan for him. Within days, my father started to recover. So much so that two months later, all symptoms of his disease practically disappeared. Another three months went by, and he began eating all the things he had never been able to eat and digest. Today, he is so hale and hearty that he just finished overseeing the construction of my parents' new home.

Once, as Guru Maharaj came back to the ashram after a stint of solitude, I remarked to him, 'Since you left the ashram, it hasn't rained one bit. Three months and not even a drop.'

He chuckled and said, '*Toh barish karva dete hain* (let's arrange for rain then).' He laughed a bit more, and the very next day, when I had to go see him at his cottage, I was carrying an umbrella. It was raining so heavily I couldn't even save my dhoti from getting wet.

In the past three years, the most important thing I have learned is to simply go along with what he says and does. Whenever he wants your opinion, he asks for it. At all other times, it is better to just follow what he says. It always pans out in the end. Always. This one time, he asked me to check with Rajivji, our ashram administrator, if the contents of the ashram building's insurance policy had been upgraded since new structures were being added almost every month.

'I had written to him,' he said to me. 'And he told me it would be done but that was four months ago. I have a feeling the matter has not been taken care of.'

I checked with Rajivji who told me that they were waiting for the valuation and as soon as they received it, they would update the policy. It was taking time because there were so many buildings in the ashram.

'This is not the answer I'm looking for,' Guru Maharaj said to me when I apprised him of the situation. He was not happy about it. 'Let them know that if by Friday afternoon, I don't have the upgraded policy sitting in my inbox, I'll assign the responsibility to someone who takes my word seriously.'

'Maharaj Sri,' I said, 'they told me not to worry as it'll be done very soon.'

'Not to worry? What kind of an answer is that? This ashram belongs to the devotees. Is Rajivji going to take the responsibility if there is an earthquake? This deadline is non-negotiable. Today is a Tuesday. By Friday afternoon, I must have the policy, and it must include the cover for an earthquake too.'

He reminded me again that the ashram belonged to the devotees and that we were its custodians. That it was the responsibility of the trustees to ensure that these things were in place so that in the event of a calamity or an untoward incident, the ashram could be rebuilt and we could protect the devotees' trust. 'I don't leave to chance what can be covered by planning,' he said. 'Besides, it's better to do our karma and be responsible, than to shun it and be in prayer.'

As per his instructions, I conveyed the strong message to Rajivji. On Friday afternoon, 12 February 2021, he sent Maharaj Sri the new policy. And on that very same Friday night, I was sitting on a bed that was shaking due to an earthquake. It was so bad, I had to rush outside to the open area. The news reported that an earthquake of 6.3 magnitude had hit Tajikistan and the tremors had been prominently felt in northern India.

A mere coincidence?

You decide.

The Mysterious Ways of the Universe

Irene Fabi

Forty-three years ago, I met a small group of people who were on the same spiritual path as me. I did not know them. However, my spiritual teacher told me that I must participate in the meeting. It was my first experience of such a gathering. Being the youngest person in the group made me feel a bit uncomfortable as well. They all knew more than I did. After the meeting, one of the members, a handsome man, came towards me and said, 'So it's you!' meaning that he had somehow been waiting for a long time. He had almost given up hope of finding a partner who was as interested in spirituality as him. It took me some time to realize, but Cupid had hit us both that day. After seeing each other for two years, we got married.

A happy, long, interesting, and sometimes not-so-easy, life followed. My husband, Aleandro, was a doctor (chief urologic surgeon in a hospital in Rome) and a spiritual seeker of truth with a scientific approach to things. He was aware that not everything could be explained by science and therefore, studied spiritual scriptures in a modern and scientific way, as best as he could.

Life was dedicated mostly to his work as a doctor, to our spiritual practice and talks with other people on spiritual matters. We organized meetings with trailblazing scientists and all sorts of educated minds interested in these matters. We hosted conferences for the Italian seat of the Club of Budapest, founded by the famed professor Ervin Laszlo, who had been nominated three times for the Nobel Prize. My husband acted as an international creative member, Doctor Karan Singh from India (politician, philanthropist and poet) was an honorary member and together with other 49 international personalities, scientists, artists and spiritual seekers, we convened frequently.

I did my best to follow my dharma as a wife, as a spiritual partner, supporting my husband's ideas and initiatives. He was a visionary with ideas very few people were able to understand. In 1995, we moved to the countryside in Italy, where I am currently residing.

In the spring of 2001, after a rather stressful time preparing for an important cultural event, the inauguration of the 'Arc of Planetary Consciousness', my life changed completely. It was my husband's idea to build the Arc. Our mayor and the Italian headquarters of the club had happily agreed to it. The Arc was built with stones sent by the mayors of over 110 capital cities of the world, dedicated to the Universal Human Values: Truth, Love, Righteousness, Peace and Non-Violence (Sathya, Prema, Dharma, Shanti and Ahimsa). The message for the new millenium, engraved boldly on the Arc, read: 'Live in a way that others can also live'.

At the end of that eventful evening, my husband told me that he had Parkinson's disease. Being a doctor, he had made the diagnosis himself. I was shocked and attributed it to the stress we had been under for the past few months. But the diagnosis was accurate, and we started to try all kinds of natural and complementary medicines, beginning with Ayurveda. It helped but towards the end we had to switch to allopathic treatment. We needed a neurologist to keep track of my husband's symptoms. Until the last nine months, we were able to lead a slow, but almost normal life. He had no tremors and was in no pain. My husband was aware that the end was in sight, it was steadily getting closer, and so he concentrated on himself. I asked and prayed to the Universe for this passage to happen at home and not in a hospital. So when the Universe granted my wish, I was very grateful we could experience that moment in his room, where he was loved and cared for till the very end. He left in a very peaceful manner at the age of 83. It happened in 2016.

My life changed forever. I was neither old nor young. I was 66, and had spent a lot of time being absorbed in the care of my husband.

After his death, I had help, but I did not want anybody to touch his body. I took care of everything. And then, I was sitting and thinking, staring into the void. Not tearful, just sad. Friends and family members were very supportive in this difficult time, but most of them lived far away and had their own families to take care of. I knew that I could and should only count on myself to make the right decision for my future. I had to turn inward and ask myself what I wanted to do with my life. It took me a year to settle a few material and bureaucratic things, following which I started concentrating on my own life. The only certainty I had was that I would continue on my spiritual path and dedicate time to prepare for a journey to India to fulfill my husband's last wish.

So I started doing some meditation again, continued reading books about spirituality and slowly discovered a good balance to things. Friends tried to pull me into restaurants, concerts, events—things people usually went to. I think they were afraid that I would fall into a depression because, most of the time, I declined their invitations. I know they wanted to be kind to me, but I asked them to let me experience this solitude, explaining that I was not depressed at all—staying on my own made me feel connected to my inner self and made me feel peaceful.

I was not looking for a guru. I just wanted to meditate, read and try and learn about the big questions of life, such as, 'Who am I?', 'Where did I come from and where will I go?' Simply seeking the truth and being on the right path was my daily practice. I had read and studied many books—the list would be too long to mention here—and one of the latest ones that I had come across was *Freedom of the Known* by Jiddu Krishnamurti.

One day, I was searching for something on the internet. Usually, Google throws up suggestions but on that day, it was Quora that appeared with the topmost results. This website was previously unknown to me. While looking at the answers, my eyes fell on an article titled, 'If you want to know a real enlightened Master, go to the Himalayas and look for Om Swami.'

I think it read more or less like a description about him and his ashram in the foothills of the Himalayas. Something clicked inside me, and I felt a strong desire to know more about this monk. I started looking for his books and read them all. Whenever a new one came out, I read it right away. I watched all the videos, practised all the meditations, followed Global Meditation, Swaminars, Black Lotus, os.me—basically pretty much followed anything that had something to do with Om Swami.

The more I read, the more I wanted to just board a plane and go to the ashram in the hopes of meeting Swamiji. But before organizing the trip, I had to make sure that there was a river at the ashram, or at least nearby the premises. I found out that the Sri Badrika Ashram was near a river called Giri Ganga. This was yet another sign that I had to go. But more on that later.

Getting organized for the trip was a little complicated for me as I had been living like a hermit for the last 10 years and, in the meantime, the world had changed a lot. Anyhow, my booking for a week at the ashram had been accepted. The arrangements for my travel, flight, visa, car from Chandigarh to the ashram, were all settled. Everything went smoothly. Very few people knew about my journey because most of my friends and relatives would have been worried, advising me not to travel alone, saying that it would be dangerous. But I wanted to travel alone! It was my journey. I knew I was in good hands and would be protected.

~

31 March 2019

The day started with Global Meditation at 4.30 a.m. Then, I practised my daily meditation and chanting, during which I mentally said to Swamiji that I was leaving home for the journey to India. At 8.30 a.m., the woman who sometimes helped me, and would now take care of my dog Aru, drove me to the nearby railway station. She promised to send a message three times a day—whenever she would go to feed and see Aru. I explained that I would not be able to call from the place I was going to. I had decided that I would only tell her I had gone to India after I came back home.

The train took me to Rome and then to the international airport. I had already done the check-in online, reserved a vegetarian meal, paid for a security pass that allowed me to fast track the screening processes. After various passport controls, security checks and a lot of walking, I got on the plane which finally took off after some delay.

The flight was perfect, and eight and a half hours later, we landed in New Delhi at 3.00 a.m. on 1 April. Before leaving home, I had made a promise to myself to have no expectations regarding a comfortable stay. Maybe I would get a room of my own in the ashram or I would have to sleep in the dormitory. Perhaps, Swamiji would grant me a personal meeting. Only good things can happen. This was my state of mind.

At the registration office of the ashram, two ladies and a gentleman welcomed me. It was only a few days before Sri Hari's birthday, so the ashram was quite full. They were trying to find a place for me, asking if I would be willing to share a room with another lady. I said that it was not going to be a problem for me. Someone accompanied me to the room. A graceful elderly lady was standing outside looking at me with frank curiousity. Her name was Mrs Sarala Panchpakesan, a very well-known and loved devotee of Om Swamiji. She said that we should be ready by 5 p.m. to go to the temple for the evening celebrations. I followed her instructions as I did not know anything about life in an ashram, about the chanting, the ways of behaving in a temple and the like.

Saralaji and her companion, Mr Ramachandran, treated me like a family member. I was so loved, I felt like I had been adopted. I'll be eternally grateful for their kindness and wonderful help. We spent some beautiful days together and still keep in touch. They will always have a place in my heart.

In the evening, during dinner, I was sitting by myself when a young, beautiful lady, all dressed in white, sat next to me. She asked me where I was from, how I came to know about Om Swami and so on. She was also very kind. I learned that her name was Sushree Diya Om. Later, I discovered that white robes meant she was training to become a nun one day. Most renunciants in the ashram have to go through white robes first and then, depending on their growth and other factors, they may be initiated into renunciation. She told me that she was born and raised in London and now lived in the ashram. I had so many things to learn.

2 April 2019, 10 a.m.
My personal meeting with Om Swami

As I entered the meeting room, my heart beat accelerated. For Swamiji was sitting like a resplendent, smiling Buddha. Though

I did my best to keep it under control, his compassionate gaze was my undoing. He asked if my stay was comfortable. I said that I was very happy and that everything was wonderful—the people, the room, the food, the place. I just felt happy and grateful.

I told Swamiji about my husband's last wish, the reason I had travelled this far. He had wished for his ashes to be dispersed in a river called Chitravati. That river, however, had run dry. Therefore, I was seeking Swamiji's permission to do the same at the river Giri. Back when Aleandro was alive, he had always wished he had been born in India, hence this was his last request. Swamiji gave me his permission and also told me to do it on Thursday, 4 April as it was a special day. I asked if I could chant the Gayatri Mantra while performing this rite. It was the only mantra I knew.

Deep in my mind, I was hoping someone could help me as I practically knew nothing about these customs.

Swamiiji, as if reading my mind, said, 'Don't worry, I'll ask Swami Vidyananda to accompany you and chant the names of the Mother Goddess as you immerse the ashes in the river.' I was so touched at this gesture. Now, all I wanted was to receive blessings from this divine being. There was silence for a few moments as I mentally prayed to him for the same.

'Step forward,' he suddenly said to me. 'I'll place my hand on your head and give you a blessing.'

It felt like it was the most important day of my life. My heart melted at his divine darshan. This was the beginning of my story, of coming home, of my life. I was floating, not walking.

The next morning, somebody told me that Sadhviji (Sadhvi

Vrinda Om) wanted to speak to me. She was waiting with her parasol near the bookshop. She informed me that we would go together with Swami Vidyananda for the little ceremony at the river tomorrow at 1 p.m. I felt a surge of emotion and gratitude for Swamiji. He had remembered and had sent a message through Sadhviji. I will never forget her big, beautiful dark eyes, her smile or her kindness.

~

The next day, the celebrations for Sri Hari's birthday commenced at the temple. Om Swamiji and Sri Hari were both beautifully adorned.

At 1 p.m., Sadhviji, Swami Vidyananda and I went down to the river. It was a warm, sunny day. As we stepped into the river's shallow end, Swami Vidyananda, in his vibrant and beautiful voice, chanted a devi stotra. Sadhviji stood near me holding my hand, while with the other, we slowly poured the ashes into the running water coming down from the Himalayas. The ceremony was special and very touching. It was as if the ashes were being carried over to the abode of the Divine Mother and merging at Her delicate feet.

I was certain my husband was pleased, wherever he may be. And I felt free, having concluded his last wish. I don't know if he'll be reborn on this planet. But if he does, it will be in India. He always said that in India, he felt at home. After the ceremony, Sadhviji splashed some water at Swami Vidyananda and me, we splashed back and soon we were all laughing. Within moments, the slight tension, the moistness in our eyes, was all gone. It was all so wonderful. I felt a little dazed. I was just a stranger in the ashram. Nobody knew me here, but with Swamiji's grace, I had received so much love and care. The next few days just flew by. The journey back home was smooth and without issues. With each passing day, my connection to Om Swamiji grew stronger in my heart.

In fact, my connection to him was so strong, I wanted him to be my guru. Meanwhile, I heard that he would be in London for a two-day meditation retreat. I decided to attend it. In London, Diyaji (Sushree Diya Om) and her wonderful, loving family threw open the doors of their home. On the first day, Swamiji arrived at the appointed time, sharp at 10 a.m. We all sat silently for 20 minutes. There were over 200 people in the room and pin drop silence; the air was full of energy. Swamiji led a guided meditation session and imparted teachings full of wisdom and humour.

My personal meeting was scheduled after the group meetings. When I entered the hall, a smiling Om Swamiji was sitting on a couch. I went rushing towards him as I didn't want him to wait, but he steadied me by saying, 'Easy.' I prostrated at his divine lotus feet and received a blessing. Looking at me, he said something very beautiful and very personal. So I summonded the courage to ask if he wanted to be my guru. 'You have already taken me as your guru and I've already accepted you. Only the formality remains. But first, a little vision awaits you,' he said mystically.

He agreed to initiate me formally at our next meeting. To say that I was happy would be an expression far too meagre to describe my state.

The next day, the meditation course started again at 10 a.m. I sat in the front row. While I was looking at Swamiji, something strange happened. His form changed and he was covered with a golden aspect—a halo. His face was different too. I thought it was Lord Vishnu. I didn't know what Lord Vishnu looked like, but this was the thought that appeared in my mind. I had seen Sri Hari, but I would not know until much later that the vision was a combined form of Lord Vishnu and the Mother Divine. Besides, the vision I was now getting was an extraordinary form that evoked unknown sentiments and devotion in me. To make sure it was not my imagination, I turned my head to one side (something I had learned in a class on spiritualism) and then looked straight ahead. He was still a golden Vishnu. I didn't know what to make of it. My longing for Swamiji became stronger and so did my wish to go back to the ashram. I decided to travel to India again. The ashram was open in October and I booked my stay for eight days.

On arriving at the ashram, I realized it wasn't crowded. People would start arriving over the next two to three days for the Diwali celebrations. I was now more familiar with the place, the temple, and had already made some friends.

On Tuesday, 22 October 2019, I had my personal meeting with Om Swamiji. I hesitated to remind him about the initiation, and started to talk about something else, but Swamiji himself brought up the topic. I can't say that I was surprised because I feel that he doesn't need to read your mind, he is in your mind. In my experience, you just have to go and be in his presence or merely think about him and the answers reveal themselves. In the past, he has not only read my mind but has also granted my wishes.

The next day was scheduled for my initiation. Upon

entering the meeting room, I knelt in front of Swamiji. What Om Swamiji told me is sealed in my heart. I won't even wonder how he knew those things. What I have come to understand is that whatever he says, comes to pass. I have realized that his words are never hollow.

I am very lucky and my life is blessed and protected. It seems that there has always been a subtle force guiding me towards a certain path; it always happened without a struggle, and now, finally, I have reached my divine master, my beloved guruji, my Swamiji. I am so grateful to the Universe for guiding me to this true and enlightened soul. I felt, in the very first moment of our meeting, that Swamiji was a divine energy in a human body. I am eternally grateful to him for having accepted me.

My life has changed, my priorities have changed, my gratitude has grown together with my happiness. My values are compassion, truth and no judgment. I hope I will have more time to stay at the ashram and be of some help in some way. I don't know what my future holds, but I know that Swamiji and Sri Hari will always be near me.

The End of a Sceptic

Sadhvi Vrinda Om

*L*ooking back, if I could choose a moment that really knocked the wind out of my scepticism's sail, it would be the day when Shamata Ma was initiated on the morning of 30 November 2015. I remember not being too surprised when the news of her sannyasa deeksha (renunciation) reached my ears.

'*She must be 65 years of age*,' the right time to don the ochre, I had stupidly thought. She certainly had the hair for it—white and long and flowing past her waist. Her eyes, though tired, had always been full of reassurance on her gentle and lined face. I was happy for her and looked forward to congratulating her when I saw her during the day. Since it was Swamiji's 36th birthday, he was expected to arrive at the small meeting room at around 8.30 a.m.

I had just put on my earrings when I heard some people holler, 'Swamiji is here.' I still had to comb my hair, which was wet from the shower, and have one last look in the mirror before I could dash out. Back then, I was neither a sannyasi nor did I have any inclination to be one. It was a few minutes before I reached the meeting room, which was by then filled with nearly 100 people. The room was a little bigger than a store-room and it was packed to its full capacity. They couldn't even shut the mesh door as people were standing on the threshold to get a glimpse of their beloved guru and to hear his divine voice. Everyone was there, soaking in Swamiji's presence, except for two latecomers who stood outside sheepishly. I found myself standing next to Manik Gautam (one of Swamiji's favourite devotees, much adored by everyone around), who assured me that there was no space to step in. We stood there straining our ears to catch what Swamiji was saying. In the next instant, the following words reached my ears.

'We'll all address her as Ma Shamata. Though I've initiated her today, I gave her my darshan many years ago. This body was 24 years old then.'

My jaw just dropped. 'You heard that, Manik? Did he say he gave her darshan that many years ago? Oh my God...' Manik shushed me up so we could hear what else Swamiji was saying. But I was no longer listening. My mind was too busy putting two and two together. I had already been living in the ashram for over a year by then and was familiar with Swamiji's ability to read minds and know the present or the past of complete strangers. What was shocking about this particular situation was that no one other than Ma Shamata could know what Swamiji meant by that statement. No one except me.

You see, a couple of months ago, I had visited Ma who at the time was Archana Claire and lived in Solan. I had some urgent paperwork that I needed her help with. She very kindly asked me to spend the night and leave for the ashram the next morning, as crossing the river in the dark wasn't safe. Those were the days when the ashram road with its curved turns scared the taxi drivers away. After a hearty meal, she made two glasses of kehwa, and I got to know a little more about her—her trials and tribulations and the things that had made her so content and graceful in life. I felt sad when I heard that, not so long ago, she had raised three children all by herself in a house where her mother had died from Alzheimer's.

A decade earlier, Ma Shamata had lost her eldest son Hariman to a degenerative disease. Her entire youth had been spent caring for and carrying Hariman from one doctor to another, one country to another, to find a treatment that would save him. She ran from pillar to post with little money and support. When her son finally seemed healthy enough and was starting out with his life and career, he quietly passed away in his sleep. He was in his early 20s. With his death, she too lost her will to live. This was the darkest chapter of Ma's life.

In her own words,

> It was 11 o'clock in the morning of 12 January 2004. My son's dead body was about to be taken away for the last rites. My heart was broken, shattered beyond repair.
>
> I tightly held on to the Bhagavad Gita, scanning its pages, hoping for some miracle, something, anything that would bring my Hariman back. Though my eyes were stinging, they no longer shed hot tears. I kept reading the passages of the Gita. My loved ones thought my grief had driven me mad. I had been reading the Gita

for three days. I had neither bathed nor changed my clothes during that time.

On that morning, a soft, silvery reflection, like that from a lamp, jumped out of the pages of the Gita. He stood before me—a youthful Brahmin in a white dhoti, with padukas, janeu and a tuft. His glance was kind and loving, radiant beyond words. Just for a few seconds, it felt as if I wasn't there. But what I was seeing was very much real; my eyes were open. I got up from my asana and said to him, "Oh Lord Vishnu has come." The Brahmin apparition smiled and said, "I'll see you in due course," and disappeared before my eyes. Once again, I was left on my own. It felt strange and then everything went quiet. It was that vision that finally gave me the strength to get up and perform Hariman's last rites.

The incredible thing was that I had clearly seen what that person had looked like, and my eyes kept searching for that visage. However, he was nowhere to be seen. Whether it was a person in a white robe, saffron robe, normal clothes—no one matched that face. No one matched that voice. And then in 2013, without any planning whatsoever, I found out about the ashram and Swamiji. I had never met him, seen him or heard about him until then. A friend of mine was going and she asked if I wanted to join. When I reached the premises, I saw that a discussion was going on at the ashram. I took one look at Swamiji and completely lost myself.

My heart was racing and my tears flowed uncontrollably. The divine being that I had looked for in various parts of India was so close to my own home?

> I went back to my house but all I could think of was Swamiji. His face didn't fade from my memory even for a moment.

Ma had narrated this incident to me serenely—as if it had happened to someone else. She had remembered every tiny detail of that day. I don't remember if I hugged her back then, but I dearly hope I did. This was the beginning of Ma's journey and it finally ended when she came to Sri Badrika Ashram nine years later. It was then she realized that the manifestation of the Brahmin that had appeared to her on that fateful day and the Swami she saw in front of her were the same. It was the same Buddha-like face that radiated peace and calm. She had seen him before. At that point, I didn't know whether I believed that it was Swamiji she saw all those years ago, or it was just something she thought to be true.

'Ma, have you ever told Swamiji about this vision? You should,' I had pushed.

'I never bother him with my sad stories. I can barely speak in front of him, his divinity. He doesn't need to hear this.' She gently shook her head and that was the last of that conversation.

On that cold November morning in 2015, as devotees wished Swamiji a happy birthday, I stood outside, shell-shocked and furiously mulling things over in my head, 'Did Swamiji really say that he had appeared to Ma Shamata all those years ago?'

How could he? Back then, he wasn't even a sannyasi but a young man of 24, running his own business.

What stumped me wasn't that Ma had never told Swamiji about the incident, and he had knowledge of it anyway. The fact that he said that it had indeed been him was what truly boggled my mind. For one thing, by then, I was certain that Swamiji abided by his vow of truthfulness at all times and at all cost. Truth was what powered his penance in this world and the next.

And so, if he said he had given Ma his vision in January 2004, under those extraordinary circumstances, then it was nothing but the truth.

This was my first experience of learning to cope with the magnitude of what Swamiji could do for the dead and the living. The seed of belief that nothing was impossible for him—that he could cut through time and universal consciousness at will—was well into the ground. A year later, he would give me details about my late mother that utterly defied what I believed about life and death. But that's a story for another time, another book, for I have too many stories and too little time on this planet to tell them all.

As for Ma Shamata, there hasn't been a more steadfast and committed disciple of my guru than her. She has stood for days in unbearable heat, picking rocks and pebbles from the ground with her own hands, readying it for fresh grass and saplings that were to be sown before her master returned from his solitude. Not many people would know this, but Ma has sat outside government offices to get approvals and sanctions for months so that all of us living in the ashram could have better amenities. She is truly a mother to those who seek her out, unconditional in her love and support of those wayward children who need her. She's extraordinary, like her most extraordinary guru.

Which brings me to another very beautiful facet of my

revered guru.

He has always given the women disciples as much respect as the men. He doesn't just worship the vigraha (form) of the Mother Goddess in our temple but also sees Her reflection, the sacred feminine, in every woman. There's no discrimination in his eyes—any seva, any service is allocated simply on competence and competence alone.

Sadhvi Shraddha, another accomplished disciple and an intelligent and competent person, was given the prestigious task of handling Swamiji's personal finances in 2017. He had chosen to give her this service over the male disciples because of her impeccable knowledge of financial affairs. Her experience of nearly 20 years in the insurance and banking industry and her trustworthiness made her the most likely candidate. Such has been her devotion to her guru that, over the years, there has been no problem too complex that Sadhviji couldn't handle. Swamiji often fondly refers to her as, 'Chandika,' a form of the Goddess that represents the power of shakti; wherever there is a situation that requires firmness and decisiveness, she is the first to take action.

On that note, I remember an anecdote from not so long ago. The morning arti had just finished and it was time for my morning japa (chanting). I was placing my asana in the sanctum-sanctorum near the lovely idol of Sri Hari, when an ugly spider sprang from behind my asana. Oh, how loudly I had screamed! It was as if a king cobra had stood at my feet and not a teeny-weeny spider. I had felt a twinge of embarrassment for spoiling the peace that had pervaded the quiet temple and its now puzzled inhabitants, but it was short-lived. The spider had parked itself on my asana, giving me the creeps, which led to me exercising my vocal cords some more. I looked helplessly at the other disciples, for someone to get me out of my predicament. But they just smiled at me. Suddenly, Sadhvi Shraddha stepped forward and with one swift, graceful movement, wrapped the spider in a cloth. She said to me jokingly, 'These kinds of tasks always come to me.' And I smiled and thought to myself, '*Yes they do. You are the brave warrior, Sadhviji. And a beautiful, fun-loving and kind person.*'

Whether it's Ma Shamata, Sadhvi Shraddha or a handful of female disciples in the white robe, an avant-garde designer, a psychologist or a programmer, Swamiji treats each and every one with respect and gives them the opportunity to apply their skill set to their fullest potential. As far as our ashram goes, there is no glass ceiling.

The Divine Mother's palpable energy in our guru's presence is no mystery. He sees Her in all women and treats us like a Devi.

The Last Word—Sadhana

On 5 March 2021, Swami Vidyananada and I served Swamiji his mid-day meal and left him to eat in peace. It was a sunny day; the Sun god shone bright and fierce, diffusing the nippy weather. We returned with the second serving five minutes later, only to find Swamiji pointing to some unusual activity on the mountains that lay further ahead to the left of the river Giri. Through the high glass walls of Swamiji's newly built cottage, we saw a cloud of smoke rising, piercing the heart of the vast blue sky.

'Some Einsteins have lit a fire again,' said Swamiji, 'This can be so dangerous, given that the forest fire can spread to their homes.'

The fires are not unusual in these parts as every year the village folk ready their fields for a new crop by burning the old one. The fire in front of us was meant to clear the field but it was beginning to consume trees, shrubs and foliage, driving the animals and birds away.

On that windy afternoon, the tall glass windows of Swamiji's cottage rattled noisily. The trees swayed in wild abandon and dry, fallen leaves floated high in the air. Fall was here and after the biting cold of winter, we couldn't have asked for anything more. But the joy of the pleasant afternoon was spoiled by the smoky sky that looked like it was rising from the mouth of a volcano spitting lava.

We watched helplessly as the same wind that made the leaves dance, fanned the blazing flames. In a span of a few minutes, the fire started to spread rapidly through the forest, up the valley of lush green trees. Swamiji immediately sent out instructions to apprise the forest department of the wildfire. His concern for the wildlife, little birds and trees took precedence over his lunch.

Around that time, Swamiji's PA, Vidu Swami (Swami Vedananda) as he's fondly called, arrived. We had all but forgotten that he had been invited for coffee and cake post Swamiji's lunch. He was most surprised to find us all glued to our seats, witnessing the intense smoke and spreading fire in front of us. By now, the flames had turned into a tornado, a screen of black smoke, thick as the kind that comes out of an industrial chimney, clouding the sky.

Seeing the mountains aflame and well past saving by human intervention, I urged our guru to do something.

'Swamiji, please stop the fire,'

'It isn't as easy, Sadhviji,'

I understood what Swamiji meant. It wasn't humanly possible to douse the fire at the height at which the mighty mountains proudly stood. I was certain the state forest department didn't have the resources at their disposal to put out a fire of such magnitude.

But being in Swamiji's service for eight years, I knew he could very well bring on rain if he so wished. Both Swami Vidyananda and Vidu Swami stood in attention and just a little nervous, for their guru had a serious expression on his face. The pleasant afternoon coffee was now a distant dream as Swamiji's demeanour had changed from jovial to sombre.

'Swamiji, you must do something! Oh, please make it rain! At this rate, the horrible fire will burn down the green forest,' I pleaded.

Pointing a finger towards the clear sky, he replied, 'It's not possible to bring rain right away as there are no clouds. We'll have to wait.'

Not willing to give up so easily, I continued to plead with him. Having witnessed countless feats where he had subdued the forces of Nature, I knew this could be done. Like a pet parrot, I carried on pestering my master to douse the fire. In my book, *Om Swami: As We Know Him*, I've narrated a passage where Swamiji turned the face of the flames in a second, like one flicks a switch. So I knew that he could do anything. Which by the way is my go-to line to him, whenever he refuses me something, I say, 'Swamiji, you can do anything. Anything at all.'

Without uttering a word, Swamiji rose from his recliner and stood with his hands crossed at the chest, quietly gazing at the tall flames and rising smoke in the distance. For a long moment, his eyes never left the burning sight in front of us. His lips moved silently. He was chanting a mantra. He turned to us and said gravely, 'All right, let's review the situation in 30–35 minutes'. I quickly asked Vidu Swami the time. It was 12.35 p.m.

Along with Swamiji, we all stepped out in to the balcony to have a better look. Oh, the strong wind that greeted us nearly threw me off balance. The smoke from the fire had exploded in the sky like a bomb going off. If the damage to flora and fauna wasn't enough, there stood a few houses that could easily be the fire's next morsel. The wind blew carrying the fire forward, swinging it high like a child in his mother's strong arms.

We stepped back in. The stillness inside the cottage was unlike the windy storm outside. Once we were all in, Swamiji spoke in his deep voice, 'The wind isn't helping our cause. To put out the fire, we first have to manage the wind.'

Only a few minutes had passed since he made that statement, when the wind started to slow down. It slowed and slowed and came to a stand-still.

'Oh my god, this is unbelievable…' I said out loud.

The glass windows stopped rattling, and everything fell quiet—not a single leaf moved on the trees nearby. Mother Nature had fallen silent in a matter of few minutes. I asked for the time—it was 12.44 p.m. The next 25 minutes passed as if I was in a dream as I constantly monitored the fire. It was like being part of an edge-of-the-seat thriller, with Swamiji sitting quietly, staring unblinkingly at the fire.

To our utter disbelief, by 1.05 p.m., the fire had all but gone out, like a bonfire gone cold with only the embers as its remains. The smoke-ridden sky, all black and grey, began to reveal shades of blue and white.

During those 30 minutes, it felt as if the fire had been vaporizing or disappearing down some secret hole in the ground. At one point during that half hour, the flames were taller than the trees on the surrounding mountain peaks. Not only that, it had spread over a few kilometres, turning everything in its way to ash. From that distance, I could see the disfigured mountains. And yet, it was there right in front of me—my master, stilling and willing the fire to die down with his glance. Exactly 35 minutes later, it was all but put out as Swamiji had said it would.

All this while, Swamiji sat in his recliner quietly listening to an old devotional song originally composed by the legendary saint-poet Surdasa. The song is about a small bird who requests God to save her life as she is in imminent danger. Swamiji had visited Varanasi a few months earlier and the devotees there had organized a small kirtan for him. As he listened to the song, he explained the meaning to us. The tiny bird is crying out to Lord Narayana, 'O Lord, please come rescue me. I seek your refuge. On one side, a hunter has his arrow aimed at me and on the other, an eagle is perched on a nearby branch ready to prey on me.'

It was the perfect song, perfect for that moment, for on that day Swamiji saved countless birds and trees, wild creatures and homes of nearby villagers, who were completely clueless of the miracle that had just taken place. Life in the ashram was the same; no one knew what had transpired, except for the disciples who had been present at the site of the miracle.

Remember, I had mentioned at the beginning of the book that Swamiji always says, 'I don't say, I just do.' This is precisely what I had meant.

Many times, over the years, I've wondered about the nature of my guru's miracles—what is it that powers his blessings? How does he will Mother Nature to yield? He's so unassuming and yet, so powerful. Gentle and powerful. Invincible, in my eyes. The answer to these questions has varied with the passage of the years and as I've grown spiritually (with my guru's grace alone), my understanding of his mystical nature has metamorphosized.

When my guru utters a sacred chant, an ancient mantra, to invoke the elements of Mother Nature, they rush to do his bidding. They mark their presence in his court. These words may appear grandiose to a mind whose belief in God and saints is limited to a bookish knowledge. But they hold true. It's a truth that I have witnessed. And I hope someday, you do too.

Another question that comes up is that can anyone chant a mantra and, over time gain, such insight into the workings of nature?

Yes and no.

I've been chanting mantras for five years and I certainly can't do what my guru does, nor have my fellow disciples obtained such unique powers.

What sets Swamiji apart from us is his penance, his sadhana. The source of his unlimited power are his spiritual practices performed over decades with intense discipline, detachment and love for every sentient being in his heart.

There's no mumbo-jumbo, no unnecessary mystique or mystery here. It's plain hard work. In meditating upon the Divine form of Lord Narayana and the Para-shakti, he has gained communion with the Universe. Sometimes, we, his disciples, catch glimpses of the Divine too as we walk upon the trail set out by our guru.

In walking in his footsteps, in calling out to the Mother of the Universe with the same fervor as our master, we realize that this path is for anyone who is not afraid to lead a spiritual life—whether they live in an ashram or in the outside world.

Sadhana and sadhana alone, my friend, is the path to fulfillment and liberation while we are alive. That's the inspiration I draw from my down-to-earth guru, simple in his living and teachings.

As his body turns 42, one that houses a soul that is trillions of years old, I place this small offering at his divine feet.

> Thank you for everything, Swamiji.
> I felt You, Lord
> A smiling presence
> You bore right into my heart
> Now the dusk of my life
> And the dawn of my soul
> I lay at your feet
> From dusk till dawn
> You reign supreme.

An Exclusive with Om Swami

Our humble obeisance at your divine feet, Swamiji. Thank you for allowing us this opportunity to interview you, especially when you have been so reclusive in the past couple of years.

For the benefit of our readers and audience, I'd like to give a little background.

When we first presented the manuscript of *The Rainmaker* to Rupa Publishers, their MD, the dynamic Kapish Mehra, immediately took on the project but with one condition—we would have to include an exclusive interview with Swamiji. He greatly admired Swamiji's simplicity of writing and thought, and believed this to be an unmissable opportunity.

Swami Vedananda and I were a bit hesitant as the book was supposed to be revealed at a surprise presentation to our guru on his 42nd birthday in November. But we figured, it would still be a surprise as knowing about the book isn't the same as knowing what is in the book.

And so, on the beautiful rainy morning of 12 July 2021, Swami Vedananda and I, Sadhvi Vrinda, virtually interviewed our most revered and venerable guru, Om Swami.

Conversation with Om Swami

Q.: Swamiji, by no means are you an ordinary person—the stories in the book speak for themselves. Then why do you insist that you are a simple sadhu in a complex world?

Ans: While I'm not exactly sure what these stories are, I can try and address this question. I think I may have some insight into human nature. But when it comes to real people, I am clueless (laughs). And that is why I say, I am a simple sadhu in a complex world because to this day, I am constantly surprised by how things sometimes unfold in our world. Or how people respond to the issues that go on in their lives. I don't think anybody can say 'I have figured out the world.' It's like a game of chess—you can master it, but you cannot conquer it. It's just one of those things where I feel that the easiest way to cope with this world is to just be simple.

Mind you, simplicity is not easy: it has a price, so to speak. If you are simple, sometimes you are taken advantage of, or people misunderstand you because this world can be a cold and an unpredictable place. When it comes to living and comprehending all that goes around me, what I have discovered, as many others might have, is that this world is far too complicated for me. Rather than try and make sense of everything, I just like to do my job quietly, surrender to the world of Mother Divine, continue to play in her lap and revel in the ignorance that comes from being a child.

I have never thought of myself as anything other than ordinary. There are people smarter than me, more intelligent, more insightful and more educated in every sense of the word. So if anything…I am below the ordinary. Because with each day of your life, you realize there is so much more to learn, so much more to be, to figure out and so much more that one can do for the world. We can do a lot more to make this existence and this planet more beautiful. Although, no contribution is going to be more than a speck of dust in the vast ocean. Let's just say if you were to put a tiny grain of sand on a beach, nobody would even notice. It's just one of those things. Therefore, one thing that I never lose sight of, ever, is that the world was just fine before I came into it. The world is going to be just fine, irrespective of whether I am here or not.

If you take the example of the pandemic (and Vidu Swami knows this), we must have turned down at least a couple hundred of interviews, events and invitations or so in the last two years. But the world is trudging on just fine. And if I was never born, or hadn't been born yet, or if I leave my body tomorrow, the world will be just fine.

So any perceived sense of extraordinariness in me for sure, and in many others, is nothing but an illusion. This is why I say, I am a simple sadhu in a complex world. When people come to me for advice or suggestions, I don't always know what to tell them. So I just say, look, Mother Divine will do as she sees fit.

Q.: Swamiji, in your simplicity we have seen divinity. But the truth is, you are a well-read, modern-day sadhu who gave up a multimillion-dollar business in the IT business and a luxurious life in the West to perform intense penance in the Himalayan woods. Why was that necessary, seeing that you are now back in the same material world?

Ans: To be honest with you, I feel a little overwhelmed as I say this. I did what I thought was the right thing to do at the time, so I could fully give myself to my spiritual journey with my Divine Mother. One of the things I wrote in my memoir was what this Bhairavi Maa, whom I had met in passing in one of the caves, had said to me, '*Beta, raja ho aur raja ki tarah rahogey.*' (son, you are a king and will live like one, forever). And I didn't think much of it, but such is the grace of Divine Mother that when I returned from the caves, and most people know this part, I lived in a tiny mud hut with practically nothing else. During my journey, I went through starvation, extreme physical austerities and challenges, basically experiencing what it felt like to have Mother Nature pick you apart, so to speak. Then a few years passed, and I had lived in the utmost physical poverty. It was…I mean…things that are taken for granted, like buying a bottle of water for example, even those proved to be a challenge. To live without electricity and running water and without any amenities and all that. But today…it's not that I have really worked towards this life, but I just kept doing what I had to do. And Mother Divine has once again brought opulence into my life. I don't know what to say about that. Should I say I am grateful…I don't know. I do this work without taking any donations and without raising funds for any of my personal needs. It's just what happens when you are simple-hearted. Because as you mentioned, you've seen divinity in simplicity. Now, you saying that is only your kindness. But the truth is, divinity *only* lives in simplicity. In complicated things, there may be ostentatiousness, there may be a projection of divinity, but real divinity is in simplicity.

Simplicity doesn't mean that you are a pauper. It means that you do not keep any clutter in your heart, mind, soul, life, while living in your world, whether it be physical, metaphysical and psychical. And it's not easy to constantly clean your house, you know? It's not spring cleaning. It's not something you do once a year, and say, okay, now my house is clean. You clean with your mind, with your inner world. It's an everyday thing. You have to clean out. But I am very grateful to the universe because you can do more when you are living comfortably. So today, once again She has blessed me with everything I need to do my job effectively, and then some.

To be honest with you, in a way, I think I am living more comfortably now than I used to when I was running a business (smiles). This work is something I deeply connect with. It resonates with me and it helps many others, which is really fulfilling for me.

Q.: What is the source of your healing? What is this energy that powers the healings and blessings that you so unassumingly bestow upon someone who seeks your help?

Ans: Two things come to mind while answering this question. First, you know in the olden days, when a servant of the king or queen would go running to deliver a message for them? Sometimes, they would take off their jewellery, a necklace or a pearl, and hand it over to the messenger. I mean, the servant would just convey a good message, that was their only contribution. Just like that, I am a servant of the Divine Mother. I just happen to be there, at the right place or at the right time. The Divine Mother wants to send a pearl or necklace to someone, and I am just the messenger. I have said this so many times, but people out of their love and devotion keep giving me the credit, and then I don't know what to say. I don't deserve their praises.

Second, what comes to my mind is a chaupai (a quartet) that I have quoted many times in the past as well, *'jania charaju karu manmahi, sut tapte dur lab kachu nahi, tap bal tej jag srijayi vidhata, tap bal Vishnu bhay pari tata, tap bal shambhu karahi sanghara, tapatey agam naahi achu samsara.'* In this verse, taken from the *Ramcharitmanas* by Goswami Tulasidas, is a story of a king and a man pretending to be a tapasvi, who says that, 'nothing is impossible with sadhana and it is with sadhna alone that Brahma created the world, it is with sadhana alone that Lord Vishnu is running this world and it is with sadhana that Lord Shiva completes the cycle of creation.' Nothing is impossible with sadhana.

And when we talk about sadhana, it is absolutely fundamental to understand that to go through it, one has to be simple-hearted, clear-hearted, pure-hearted and humble. Not just polite, but humble. These are the rewards of proper sadhana. Without this, anything is but an *attempt* to do sadhana, not the actual sadhana. Till the time that we have false pride or believe ourselves to be different or to be different or special, sadhana can never be attempted and consequently, it cannot heal. Healing is something only the Divine does. Only Mother

Nature can truly heal. I am simply someone who is getting the opportunity to deliver the right messages. And that is the truth and that is what I feel in my bones. I am not saying this to humour someone or to appear a certain way. This is what I actually feel every single day.

Q.: It's difficult for an educated mind to wrap their head around the word, 'sadhana'. Most people neither have the time nor the inclination to understand it. What can you say that can motivate and encourage people to go back to their roots and perform chanting and meditation as our ancestors once did in this holy land?

Ans: As they say, nothing motivates like success. Sadhana is hard, but so is working out in the gym, cleaning your home, cooking, doing your daily chores, washing dishes or ironing your clothes. It's the after-effects that motivates us. With sadhana too, I say, start small but stick with a practice and don't give up. Most importantly, cultivate the virtues in your life and maintain the equanimity of the mind as well. The situation works both ways—you do sadhana and you are blessed with some virtues; you cultivate some virtues and you are blessed with some sadhana. So these practices complement each other. Like I always say, it doesn't matter what you are doing, just stick with it, keep improving the quality of that practice and keep becoming a better human being. Unfortunately, most of the self-help books of today teach us extreme self-centeredness. They are full of advice like 'oh you are very special,' 'you need to love yourself.' (laughs) I mean, everybody loves themselves, and when you tell people things like, 'be compassionate with yourself,' 'love yourself,' 'accept yourself,' people will say yes, they have suffered a lot and they really need to love themselves and so on. Of course you need to do that, but you also need to love other people. I mean, if you really believe in the Divine Mother, why is it so hard to see Her in everybody? The truth is, it's not hard. It's just that the curtain of ego is drawn over the inner eye that prevents the individual from doing so. It's like, you can go to the gym and spend an hour there and not accomplish anything or you could go to the gym and do 15 minutes of rigorous exercise and come out all sweaty and having burned a few hundred calories. Similarly, you can sit in sadhana for two to three hours and think about all the negative things and have no impact on yourself, or you could do it in a quality fashion and see the changes for yourself. I remember, in a gym that I once visited, I came across the line, 'exercise with passion or don't do it.' So didn't do it (laughs). It's the same thing with sadhana. If you are not going to do it properly…notice how I didn't use the word seriously? For sadhana can be a very joyous affair, but it still has to be done properly and sincerely, with no shortcuts. If you are not going to do it that way, you will not see the results. The only result will be more pride, more anger, more rigidity.

Q.: Swamiji, can you please talk to the readers about the importance of sadhana and how by practicing it, one can be closer to the Divine Mother, to God? And elaborate on why it is such an important path leading to the Divine?

Ans: There are, in fact, many paths that lead to the Divine. Some are long routes and others are short. Sadhana is our definitive way of experiencing Oneness with the Universe. That is all I have to say.

Q.: Swamiji, love is an intrinsic human emotion. Why is it becoming so difficult to find it or receive it? Or to put it in another way—is love an over-hyped human emotion?

Ans: Love is an intrinsic human emotion. So is pride, jealousy, anger (laughs)...but why is love so hard to achieve? Well, it's actually not that difficult, you know? There is a saying and I have said this in the past, '*Jab main tha, Hari nahi, ab Hari hain, main nahi, sab andhiyara mit gaya, jab deepak dekha mahi*'. (When it was me, there was no Hari; when there was Hari, there was no me; all of the darkness vanished when I saw the light). The reason why love, or true love, can be a little hard to find is because you cannot really be in love unless you are one with the object of your love. And to be one with them requires that you become that object. I become them if they love me. Now if you are a rock, you cannot dissolve in milk. Maybe if it is left in some liquid for millions of years, there might be some dissolution but not much beyond that. You have to be compatible. Even if you are sugar, you have to have the desire to dissolve and drop your ego. And that's easier said than done. It's a painful process because there is such comfort in being who we have always been.

Why did I go for my own sadhana? It was to change myself, to transform myself. There comes a moment when a little bird has to tumble out from its nest so that just before it can crash to the ground, it has to spread its wings and fly. But before that moment, between the time that it comes out of the nest and the point at which it spreads its wings, there is a lot of planning, a lot of fear. Any misguided action and it could be the end for that bird. This is why love can be hard.

And is love overhyped? I think the value of love cannot be overhyped or overstated, ever. Without love, human existence has no meaning. But what is love, anyway? Saying 'I love you,' is that love? Actually, it's very rare for people to truly love somebody else. What they love is the image of the other person. They love the joy they get by building memories with the other person. If those memories are not joyous, love will diminish. And it's those memories and experiences that we are attached to it. That is the difference between human love and Divine love—the level of purity. In human love, you are attached to those beautiful experiences; you don't want to dissolve. In Divine love, you say, it doesn't matter what I am, I have to let go. Otherwise, why would Krishna say '*Sarva dharman parityaj mam ekam sharnam vraj*' (The Bhagavad Gita, Chapter 18, Verse 66). Why would he say to Arjuna, 'Just do what I tell you to do. Surrender unto me.' That's because you will not get to the next level of consciousness, you will not know what you are capable of doing, if you become complacent or keep clinging to your ways of doing things. I mean, that is what awakening is, right? A new way of loving, a new way of looking at the world, a new way of thinking, a new way of doing things. What else is awakening? Awakening means that I have been living in a certain manner, or doing things a certain way that perhaps meant that I was asleep some of the time. Sleeping through my egos, sleeping through my beliefs, sleeping through anything! Now my eyes are open, and I am seeing the world differently. That is what awakening is.

Q.: It is said, quite often, that ego acts as a hindrance to achieving the higher truth in life. But isn't ego what defines us, what makes us unique?

Ans: Ego is a very egoistic topic (laughs). Ego doesn't necessarily make us unique. It makes us *feel* we are unique. What really makes us unique is our capacity to give and receive love. What makes people unique is their behaviour, their thinking, their conduct, their nature. Ego is what makes us do things that separate ourselves from the rest of the world. Maybe it is to protect ourselves, maybe it is something we do to give ourselves a sense of progression or moving forward. If you think of yourself as an egg, then ego is the shell; you need it till a certain point before you are hatched. But once you are hatched, you don't need it. However, if someone were to break that shell before you are ready, it would be the end of you. You would become an omelette in a frying pan, you'd lose your existence and would end up in somebody's tummy. So when we take initiation, for instance, the role of the guru is to know when to break that shell. Do it too early and one can cause irreparable damage, do it too late and it's just as bad. You need to know the right moment; and here's the beautiful thing—to hatch an egg you don't attack it with a hammer or throw it, or tap it into some utensil. You just provide the right amount of warmth and give it the right time until it hatches. That is the difference between a teacher and a guru. A teacher will tell you that ego is bad. They may say, 'Go stand in a corner with both arms raised.' But the guru will say, 'Well, it is painful. I have to watch it at all times, but I must continue to provide warmth, so that, one day, this egg may hatch correctly.' It happens from the inside.

Q.: How do we connect with the Divine? Do we do so through prayers, rituals or by connecting with ourselves?

Ans: We do so through all of these. In primary school, usually every child at some point in time asks, 'What's the point of studying mathematics?' One thinks, where would they use this calculus or chemical formulas or physics and so on. What happens is that every subject you study shapes your brain a little; every subject exposes your brain to solving a problem in a slightly different manner, to consider the challenge in a different way. So if math will give you logic or analytical thinking, the humanities will give you a creative side, and make you think about other cultures, other experiences and other philosophies. Similarly, when we pray, we start with certain rituals at the beginning, or we have a certain structure to our sadhana that works on one aspect of us. Practicing the virtues of empathy, compassion, universal love, devotional service works on another aspect of your personality. Working on yourself, constantly improving yourself for 'dhyay' or self-study, reflecting on the scriptures, or reflecting on how your day has been works on yet another aspect of you. So everything is necessary.

Q.: Swamiji, nowadays, even when people look happy and project happiness, they are, at the same time, still searching for joy and contentment. Isn't that contradictory?

Ans: I think, nowadays, people are under lot of pressure to look happy and social media has a huge role to play in that. On social media, everybody is having fun—they are vacationing in nice places, they are cutting cakes every day, eating out every day (and nobody is wearing a mask). Everybody's home is a palace of joy, and there may be some truth to it...I am not saying all those pictures are fake, but the truth is that these are just snapshots of the movie. When we are seeking joy, the difference between an awakened individual and somebody who is working towards it, is fundamental. And that difference is that someone who is not fully liberated (or awakened) thinks that other people are responsible for their joy or misery. For instance, they might think that if their family behaved in a certain way, they would be happy; if their children studied in a particular way, they would be happy; if their partner did this or that, they would be happier or life would just be better. An awakened individual, instead, knows that these are just excuses of the human mind. That if we cannot be happy in this moment, we cannot be happy in any other moment. An awakened individual realizes that happiness is not somebody else's job; a person's happiness is in their custody. Due to their own ignorance, sometimes people lock away their happiness and give the key away to another person, after which they constantly look at that person for happiness! This is in complete opposition to the definition of an adult—that if you are a grown-up you are responsible for your own self. If you are an adult and you are in your car but you aren't wearing the seat belt, you are the one who is responsible, not the driver. If the policeman pulls you over, you can't just say sorry and that you didn't know the rules. Similarly, in spirituality, or in general life, there comes a moment when a person becomes a grown-up. Then you cannot treat that person like a child. It's disrespectful. So happiness is an outcome. If you run after it, you will miss the whole point. You have to know what you feel like doing or what is important to you, and happiness will come. Happiness is like a paying guest. It will come and it will go, only to come back again. Next semester, it will come back again, and give you some trouble (laughs). It's demanding, and yeah, that's about it.

The other thing I really wish I could get across to this world is that we change all the time. An honest person is the one who accepts that change and says, 'Well, you know what? I have changed. I don't feel the same way anymore. What mattered to me yesterday no longer matters to me.' When you are in your 20s, you are very easily motivated. You see a successful person and you say, 'Well, you know, I can do this business. I can do that thing. I can do that sadhna. I'll do that and I will also be successful.' In your 30s, you question yourself, 'Can I? Can I say no?' In your 40s, you say, 'Well I am happy where I am.' That last person can be wherever he wishes to be (laughs).

I don't have to be the richest person, the wealthiest or the most intelligent. I don't have to win this award or that prize. And this is liberation. The people who have worked with me know the number of times we have refused media interviews and events. The courage to say no is the first sign of liberation. Happiness cannot come by saying yes to everything because then you are a doormat. Happiness comes from a) clarity, when you know what you want to do; b) persistence, just going for your goals; c) filtering things out, which is knowing when to say no. We have somehow morphed compassion into a thing where we are forced to say yes to everything; we think we have to be liked and loved by everyone. This is simply not possible. '*Waiz bura kahen toh gila nahin Ghalib; aisa bhi hain koi jise sab accha kahen*' ('I don't mind if some call me bad,' says Ghalib, 'after all, is there anyone whom everybody calls good.') Nobody is liked by everyone they know. It is okay to have a difference of opinion, it is okay if people are not singing your praises all the time. It is okay (smiles). And that is happiness. We should try and do something creative every day. I know this rule cannot apply to everyone and I don't intend to say it's a panacea, but personally, if I do not do anything productive in a day I feel a bit irritated. I feel a sense of guilt—that nature gave me these 24 hours and I have somehow squandered them. This is also no good (laughs). I mean, you should not feel guilty for being harmless and not doing anything (laughs again). We are not machines. Personally, I feel that I should do something good for everyone each day. And that is happiness for me.

Q.: Swamiji, we've often heard you say, 'When truth knocks, it knocks you down.' What do you mean by this?

Ans: There are these buildings called heritage buildings. You can renovate them but you work with a lot of limitations when you work on them. You can't just shape them according to the designs of the current world, and even if you manage to restore them, they will stand for only so long, and one day, they will crumble. So one way to lead one's life is to do a bit of patchwork, to treat yourself as an antique and restore yourself every now and then. And the other way is that you decide to rebuild your life from scratch.

When truth walks into your life, it may sound very romantic, but it is, in fact, painful because the first thing it does is burst your bubble. And when the bubble bursts, you feel lost. The truth is an extreme makeover. And that is why I say, 'When truth knocks, it knocks you down' because it forces you to step out of your illusions. In the book *The Last Gambit*, I wrote something like, 'Life is not a game of chess, it has no rules per se and when it comes at you, in one blow it slaps you out of your illusions'. And while it is painful, the effects are not just liberating, but deeply empowering too.

Q.: You have always shied away from being idolized and have always given credit to hard work and self-discipline for your accomplishments, whether in business or in the spiritual world. You have always maintained that there are no shortcuts in life. What in your view should we strive to achieve—a successful life or a purposeful life?

Ans: A purposeful life, for sure, because if your life is purposeful it will truly be successful. I mean, what else is success? There are cases in history where people successful in business, in entertainment and public figures, have taken their own lives because they couldn't handle it. In terms of power, wealth and fame, they had everything but they did not *feel* their success; what they had achieved was not born out of a purpose. If I have a purpose in my life, I will feel success automatically. What else is success? Success is not external validation. No, there are millions of unsung heroes who are doing great work in numerous spheres, people the world doesn't even recognize, let alone appreciate. Sometimes they don't receive any acknowledgment throughout their entire lives. But does that mean they are unhappy? Not necessarily so. As long as they feel what they are doing actually matters to them, they will be happy. And that is what success is. A life with purpose, most certainly, is the ultimate life.

And if I may say, it is perfectly fine for the purpose to change. It is okay if you once felt deeply for a cause, a purpose, a person or a guru, but no longer feel the same way. It is okay if your life's purpose is somewhat different today. In fact, this is the case with most people, but unhappiness comes when we stick with something and keep doing it just because we have been doing so for a while. Caring about what people might say despite no longer connecting with that purpose is a grave mistake. See, your time on this planet is quite short. The last thing you need is excessive baggage that you can do without. So when we truly experience a change, it is much more honest to say, 'I think my purpose in life is shifting and I feel like doing something different'. Feel free to take that call. Always have the courage to express yourself when you feel a shift in your purpose because that means that your consciousness has shifted. It can mean that nature is preparing you for something more phenomenal, that your consciousness has grown and maybe you are at the threshold of an awakening. Maybe, for the first time, you are actually close to discovering your true purpose in life. That everything until then has simply been a matter of preliminary preparation to get you to where you are today.

Q.: Where does true fulfilment come from in one's life?

Ans: So if you live only for the world, you will burn out. Those who say they only live for the world are telling themselves stories that they choose to tell themselves, stories that may not necessarily be right. Fulfillment comes from taking care of yourself, not neglecting what you fundamentally need. It is about fulfilling the purpose of your life, the purpose you feel you have and, at the same time, doing your bit for the world so that we don't injure other living beings.

What I can say without a doubt is that anyone who thinks they can be happy by hurting others is kidding themselves. Those who think that they'll only look after themselves and be happy and satisfied in life are sadly mistaken. It has to be a balance.

It's like when you are in a plane and there is an emergency and the oxygen masks drop down. It will help if you put on yours first and then move on to your co-passenger. Think about a mother, the nursing mother—if she has to feed her child, she also has to feed herself. If she doesn't, her fragile body will give up one day and she will not be able to care for herself or her children. So self-care is definitely important. Lord Krishna said, '*Karshayantah shareerastham bhootagraamamachetasah; Maam chaivaantahshareerastham taanviddhyaasuranishchayaan.*' (Those who torture themselves by neglecting the needs of the body are hurting me.) Following penances that have not even been prescribed by the scriptures is not only ignorance but arrogance. The 'I' becomes bolder and bigger and more important here, which should not be the case. Have you ever noticed the alphabet I? It stands alone, just a straight line without any curves or shape or beauty. A line at the bottom and one at the top. And if you push it, it will fall (smiles).

Q.: One of the chapters in this book is about Vanika Bansal who, with your grace, has now become an ashram resident. My question is, as with Vanika's life story, does pain, helplessness and grief lead to a spiritual path?

Ans: One of the sad truths of human life is that without pain you never realize your true potential. Pain, is necessary for spiritual growth. Now there is a self-inflicted pain, and I am not talking about that. Self-inflicted pain is just a form of suffering. I am talking about the times when life kicks us in the gut, forces us to wince and do something to escape from the pain. In fact, we often think that happiness is escaping from that pain. One way to look at happiness is to increase your pain threshold because pain is an integral part of human existence; it is inevitable. But if I increase my threshold, things that were earlier painful to me will no longer cause me any pain. It won't cause me to suffer and suffering is my interpretation of pain. Jo pukar dard mein hoti hain na, wo haas parihaas mein nahi ho sakti. (The ingenuity or sincerity of calling out to the Divine when you are in pain is of a different kind altogether.)

When the child in the next room is crying because she didn't get the toys she wanted, the mother knows. But when the same child is crying because she has stubbed her toes or has fallen from the bed, it is a different cry, and the mother knows the difference. She knows exactly when to drop everything and run to the child and when to let the child be. She knows that when there is real pain, her child needs her. So when life puts us through pain and we call out to the Divine, it transforms us. I would say nothing transforms us as rapidly as pain. It's not always positive transformation, though. Some people become bitter, some angrier and some become more insecure when they are put through pain. But the reverse also happens. Sometimes, pain makes one softer and humbler. Although, the level of pain has to be somewhat manageable—not so much that someone is broken down and not so little that the person may not feel anything. It has to be somewhere between these two extremes.

Q.: Swami Vedananda has been your personal assistant for the last three years. He's always been in awe of the fact that his Guru Maharaj places great emphasis on the small things in life. These things are so minor that they are almost invisible but actually have a huge impact on someone's personality. Do you believe that God is in the details?

Ans: I am someone who has always paid attention to the details. My mind is trained that way, I'm not even doing it consciously. And I love working with people who pay great attention to the little things, as well. Throughout my life, I cannot recall doing anything just for the heck of it. I deeply respect and admire those who do their job very thoroughly, who take it very seriously and pay close attention to everything. How important are the tiny details? It's like having the perfect amount of salt in your meal. If the amount gets messed up even by a little, the joy of the entire meal is compromised. And it is different for different people. I mean, what might be a 'detail' to me may not be the same for the other person. And that's the thing. When we care about something, when we are passionate about doing something, we automatically care about all the details, no matter how big or small. My background in computing has helped me a lot in caring for the details in life. In programming, if you miss a single semi-colon or a bracket, you'll be unable to compile the thousands of lines that you may have written; it simply won't work. I followed the same method in sadhana—I paid attention to my mind. I examined whether my mind was lucid, confused, distracted or clear. This mentality is me because otherwise I could have sat with the Rudrakasha beads all day long and chanted and chanted, and yet, would never been able to experience the Divine. It's the details that mattered. In our country, there is a tendency of saying 'ho jayega.' You know, the 'jugaad' mentality? And when things go out of hand, we panic. This is what happened during the Covid pandemic. In the beginning, we ignored the details, like wearing masks, social distancing, vaccination, etc. And the countries that paid attention to these details, were the ones that, very early on, were able to take care of their people. So the details definitely matter. You walk into a McDonald's and order a veggie burger, and it tastes the same every time. But imagine if at times, your bread was soggy or if the patty was dry or the lettuce was dead, would you feel the same way? So with Sadhana, in the very same way, if you want to replicate the experience of joy, attention to detail is paramount.

With sadhana, it goes like this—I just have to pay attention to this moment, then the next, and then the next. I may only be sitting for five minutes, but those five minutes need to be full of attentive moments. And it's different for different people. Some believe in diving into the depths—they will build a business, keep focusing on its core and develop a niche. Some believe in focusing on the breadth and like to diversify; they want to have different sources of revenue for their business. It's a question of individual preference, as long as you are perfecting the art of whatever it is that you are doing, you are paying attention to it.

Q.: Swamiji, with the Covid pandemic engulfing the world, human beings need healing now more than ever. Do you think spirituality is the way forward for broken souls and minds?

Ans: Every act can be a spiritual act. Even a country can be led spiritually. I am not talking about religiousness, but spirituality. The latter is something that always forces us to look inward, to see ourselves in the mirror without make-up, without lighting and filters, to see ourselves for who we really are. Spirituality is definitely a part of the healing process, but we also need good governance, educating people about the pros and cons of living a certain way, the right laws in place as well as the enforcement of those laws in order to emerge victorious from this pandemic as quickly as possible.

Q.: Is a life with God's presence in it more rewarding than one without it? What makes life beautiful for one person and miserable for another?

Ans: Expectations (pauses)…so definitely a life with God in it is…how do I say it…it's like if you are purely living for yourself, then your life has no God in it. It may have idols, mantras, sadhanas, but it will have no God. If your life has other people in it and you are trying to make their lives better, then you already have God in your life. And what makes one person more miserable than the other? Well, the answer is expectations. Expectations come from a sense of entitlement, which is a direct derivative of false pride. False pride is simply, intrinsically and inevitably linked to one's ego, which stems from ignorance. This inevitably means that this person is fast asleep in their bed of illusions.

Q.: What is your message to someone who aspires to be like you and follow in your footsteps? Is that even possible?

Ans: I mean, God help the person who aspires to be like me (laughs). Because one of the downsides is that they will always be working. There is no rest or relaxation in my life. And I work pretty much all day and all the time. I have said this before, I never thought that after taking monkhood it would actually be like this. Although, I am trying to take some steps to change this, and I am working on something that I am quite excited to share with the world, hopefully in a few months' time. It will be my offering to Santana Dharma, and I hope people will like what I have put together. But if somebody wishes to be like me, I don't think it's a good goal because what are they really aiming for? I mean, what aspect of me are they seeing that they would like to replicate in their lives? Yes, I am happy, I am content and I am incredibly joyous, but does that mean I don't have my sad moments? Of course I do. Does that mean I face any less challenges? Of course not. In fact, my challenges are more than what many people face in their lives; not only are they great in number but bigger in size. When we want to be like somebody, what we do is that we marry ourselves to an aspect of that person and we say, you know what, I would like to be like that person. I don't think that's a good thing.

It's okay for people to listen to me, to read what I have to say. If they like what they hear, they can adhere to the advice. If they don't like it, they can chuck it, and it's perfectly okay. I think if people need to be anything, it's that they need to be a better version of themselves because there is so much beauty and joy to be discovered in doing that. And that is the true meaning of progress. I mean, progress is not liking or starting to feel like someone. Progress is 'Am I doing better than yesterday?'

I have great respect for my own guru, Naga Baba of Kamauli, and your param guru, but I never tried to be like him. I never, for a moment, thought that, *'Yes, I should be like him.'* I have read the works of all the major saints across all the major religions, and I have never felt like, 'Oh, I wish I was like Swami Vivekananda or Ramakrishna Paramhansa,' or 'I wish I could live like Ramanna Maharishi.' No, I have never done that.

They have my greatest respect. I bow down before them and pay my greatest obeisance to them, but I am just Om Swami and I am okay with that, otherwise I will not feel fulfilled. I mean, Ramanna Maharishi lived on one mountain for his entire life! Could I do that if I wanted? Well, I am not so sure. Would I want to do it? I don't think so. And he was so sweet. Ramanna Maharishi made himself available 24x7. He gave clear instructions to his people that whenever somebody came to visit him on the mountain (Arunachala mountain) where he lived, they were to wake him up. Even if it was in the middle of the night, he would see that person. I don't have that patience or compassion. I barely see people once or twice a year. If I wanted to be like him, I know I would fail miserably. I am not built like that. I am doing the next best thing—doing the best that I can. Interactions are not my thing. It's not something I am cut out for. It has always been like that and it's the one thing that hasn't changed in me at all. So to be honest with you, the only reason I interact with people is because I have to. Not that this interview has got anything to do with that (laughs). It was really nice talking with you and answering your questions.

Om poornamadah poornamidam poornaat poornamudachyate
Poornasya poornamaadaaya poornamevaavashish yate
Hari Om Tatsat
Hari Om Tatsat
Hari Om Tatsat

❧